How to
DRINK
LIKE A WRITER

Recipes for the Cocktails and Libations
that Inspired 100 Literary Greats

APOLLO
PUBLISHERS

Visit our website at www.apollopublishers.com.

Library of Congress Cataloging-in-Publication Data is available on file.

Writing by Margaret Kaplan.
Cover and interior design by Rain Saukas.
Line drawings by Jessica Fimbel Willis.

Print ISBN: 978-1-948062-48-0
Ebook ISBN: 978-1-948062-49-7

Printed in the United States of America.

CONTENTS

BAR TOOLS

Cocktail shaker	Large mixing glass	Barspoon	Muddler

Strainer	Swizzle stick	Citrus juicer	Rocks glass or old-fashioned glass

Pint glass	Collins glass	Coupe glass	Martini glass

Shot glass	Wine glass	Flute glass	Mug

STOCKING
THE CABINET

- Absinthe (Pernod)
- Aged rum
- Aperol
- Applejack (Laird's)
- Apricot liqueur
- Armagnac
- Batavia Arrack
- Beer (stout, lager, pale ale)
- Bitters (angostura, Peychaud's, walnut)
- Bourbon
- Brandy (Cognac, calvados, apricot)
- Cachaça
- Campari
- Cherry Heering
- Cointreau
- Crème de cassis
- Crème de menthe (green, white)
- Cynar
- Disaronno Originale
- Gin
- Irish whiskey
- Kahlúa
- Kirsch
- Kümmel
- Liquore Strega
- Light rum
- Lillet Blanc
- Maraschino liqueur
- Mezcal
- Pisco
- Pine liqueur
- Port (ruby)
- Rye whiskey
- Scotch whisky
- Sherry (amontillado)
- Spiced rum
- Tequila
- Triple sec
- Velvet falernum
- Vermouth (sweet, dry, blanc)
- Vodka
- Wine (red, white, Champagne)
- Yellow chartreuse
- Żubrówka (Polish bison grass vodka)

1564 ——— 1616

William Shakespeare's
METHEGLIN

SERVES 16

In Tudor times, food and drink was celebrated for its medicinal purposes.[1] Beer, wine, and cider were enjoyed not only for their inebriating qualities, but for their purported ability to keep illness and infection at bay. Metheglin, or spiced mead, was particularly utilized as a tonic for good health. In fact, the word "metheglin" comes from the Welsh *meddyglyn*, or medicinal liquor, rooted in the Latin *medicus*.[2] Shakespeare references the fermented honey wine—a seasoned version of the oldest alcoholic beverage known to man—in *Love's Labour's Lost* and *The Merry Wives of Windsor*, and would have undoubtedly taken a tipple at the first chill, ache, or sniffle.[3]

One 2-inch piece of ginger root, unpeeled	6 whole cloves	3 pounds wildflower honey
2 lemons	1 cinnamon stick, broken into pieces	1 ounce baker's yeast

Bruise unpeeled piece of ginger by whacking it with a pan until it is slightly smashed and broken. Peel and juice lemons; set juice aside. Place lemon peel on a piece of cheesecloth with the ginger, cloves, and cinnamon stick, gather the corners together and tie with twine to form a bundle, and place in a large pot.

Add 8 pints water and the lemon juice and bring to a boil, then lower heat and allow to cool to 122 degrees F.

Add honey to the pot. Remove pot from heat and when contents cool to 70 degrees F, remove the bundle of aromatics. Add yeast and mix lightly.

Pour the liquid into the fermentation jar. The liquid should reach about three-quarters full, just below the fermentation jar's built-in air-lock. (The air-lock is the one-way valve inside the jar that allows the gases created during fermentation to escape while ensuring that the atmosphere remains air-tight and free of oxygen, preventing the formation of bacteria and mold during the fermentation process.[4])

Let ferment for 1 to 2 weeks until liquid is clear, and then transfer to bottles.[5]

Store bottles at cool room temperature for at least 4 to 6 months before serving, or better yet, let the metheglin age for several years.

1775 — — 1817

Jane Austen's
NEGUS*

**SERVES 4 TO 6 DEPENDING
ON TOLERANCE FOR
LIQUOR AND DANCING**

The lavish and long-lasting balls of Jane Austen's Regency-era London were typically fueled by ample servings of negus, a warm, spiced wine. Austen would have undoubtedly encountered and enjoyed the popular refreshment at the dances she attended; after all, negus makes appearances in *The Watsons* and in *Mansfield Park* at Fanny's celebration ball.[6] Today's social occasions might lack the ceremony, intrigue, and preoccupation with conduct that defined those of Austen's England. Still, a few cups of negus, a candelabra,

* Adapted from *How to Mix Drinks: Or, The Bon-Vivant's Companion* by
Jerry Thomas, 1862

and a pianoforte, and you might see yourself moving from the drawing room to the parlor with the pluck and fortitude of Austen's heroines, or with the understated charm of Mr. Darcy.

> As Tom Musgrave was seen no more, we may suppose his plan
> to have succeeded, and imagine him mortifying with his barrel
> of oysters in dreary solitude, or gladly assisting the landlady in
> her bar to make fresh negus for the happy dancers above.[7]
>
> —*The Watsons*, 1805

1 lemon	1 pint ruby port	Lemon slices for garnishing
2 tablespoons sugar	Fresh nutmeg, grated, to taste	

Peel lemon, being careful to avoid an excess of pith. Place lemon peel in a medium-large saucepan, then juice lemon and add juice to the saucepan. Add sugar and port and heat over medium, stirring until sugar is dissolved and mixture is hot. Meanwhile, in a separate small saucepan, heat water to a boil. When sugar has dissolved into the port, stir in a cup of hot water. Strain mixture into a pitcher and add nutmeg. Garnish with slices of lemon.

Serve negus with white soup, a Regency-era, veal-based stock that would have been the belle of every ball (and that, unlike negus, won't leave stains).

RECIPE FOR WHITE SOUP FROM JOHN FARLEY'S *The London Art of Cookery*, 1783:

Put a knuckle of veal into six quarts of water, with a large fowl, and a pound of lean bacon; half a pound of rice, two anchovies, a few peppercorns, a bundle of sweet herbs, two or three onions, and three or four heads of celery cut in slices. Stew them all together, till the soup be as strong as you would have it, and strain it through a hair sieve into a clean earthen pot. Having let it stand all night, the next day take off the scum, and pour it clear off into a tossing-pan. Put in half a pound of Jordan almonds beat fine, boil it a little, and run it through a lawn sieve. Then put in a pint of cream, and the yolk of an egg, and send it up hot.[8]

1792 — 1822

Percy Bysshe Shelley's
GREEN TEA ARNOLD PALMER LEMONADE

SERVES 1

The Romantic poet Percy Bysshe Shelley was almost a beacon of healthy living. He maintained a vegetarian lifestyle before it was cool, eschewing the animal-based staples that dominated most diets in the nineteenth century.[9] Shelley was, however, subject to a tyrannical sweet tooth on top of an insatiable appetite for caffeine.[10] Tea, especially high-quality green tea, was Shelley's favorite.[11] The poet also consumed large quantities of lemonade,[12] made sweet by honey (he was known to enjoy it straight from the honeycomb) and not sugar (which liberals and intellectuals of the time boycotted for its ties to slavery).[13] This recipe is nonalcoholic, and will leave you clearheaded for a productive day of writing. But if you are seeking more than just a caffeine buzz, you can't go wrong with the addition of an ounce—or two—of bourbon.

| 2 lemons | 2 green tea bags |
| 1 tablespoon raw honey | Mint sprigs for garnishing |

Zest and juice both lemons. In a small saucepan, combine zest and juice, 1 ½ cups filtered water, and the honey. Bring to a boil and stir to dissolve honey. As soon as honey is dissolved, remove from heat. Let cool.

Meanwhile, heat an additional 1 ½ cups filtered water in another small saucepan until it boils. Remove from heat, add green tea bags, and steep for 2 or 3 minutes. Remove tea bags and let cool.

Pour tea into a large glass jar. Using a fine-mesh strainer, strain lemonade into the same jar. Cool in refrigerator and enjoy chilled over ice. Garnish each serving with a mint sprig.

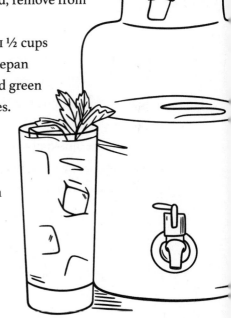

1809 — 1849

Edgar Allan Poe's
EGGNOG*

SERVES 8

Though legend holds that Edgar Allan Poe died drunk on a street in Baltimore, updated research shows that his delusions, belligerence, and rapid decline might have been caused instead by rabies.[14] Like whatever creature sunk his teeth into the famed poet and playwright, this eggnog, passed down from the Poe family, has bite—but it's more likely to leave you slumped in an armchair than encephalitic in a gutter.

---

* Adapted from the Poe family recipe from 1790

7 egg yolks

1 cup sugar

5 cups whole milk

½ cup heavy whipping cream

1 ½ cups good brandy

¼ cup dark rum

Nutmeg, freshly grated, for garnishing

Stir together egg yolks and sugar in a small bowl. In a small saucepan, warm 3 cups of whole milk over low heat. Whisk 1 cup warmed milk into egg mixture, slowly so as not to scramble. Add milk and egg mix back into the saucepan, stirring until combined. Remove from heat and stir in heavy cream. Stir off heat until mixture is cooled. Add remaining 2 cups of whole milk, brandy, and rum and stir to combine. Top with nutmeg. Drink to your telltale heart's desire, and then, as quoth the Raven, "drink some more."[15]

Sir Walter Scott and William Makepeace Thackeray's
GIN TWIST

SERVES 1

"Then," said the Captain, "Sir Bingo, I will beg the favour of your company to the smoking-room, where we may have a cigar and a glass of gin-twist; and we will consider how the honour of the company must be supported and upholden upon the present conjecture."[16]
—Sir Walter Scott, *St. Ronan's Well*, 1823

About eleven, men in white neckcloths drop in from dinner-parties, and show their lacquered boots and shirt-studs with a little complacency—and at midnight, after the theatres, the young rakes and *viveurs* come swaggering in, and call loudly for gin-twist.[17] —William Makepeace Thackeray, *Sketches and Travels in London*, 1856

Above left: Sir Walter Scott
Above right: William Makepeace Thackeray

Scottish novelist, poet, and biographer Sir Walter Scott, best known for 1819's *Ivanhoe*, is often credited as the inventor of the historical novel, lauded for a literary style that weaves lyricism, clarity, and ornateness.[18] Scott was also a keen observer of society and led an active social life.[19] No wonder, then, that he mentions the gin twist, a warm gin tipple and a common early cocktail in the nineteenth-century United Kingdom, in his 1823 novel *St. Ronan's Well.* Years later, William Makepeace Thackeray, author of *Vanity Fair* (1847–1848) and *The History of Henry Esmond, Esq.*, makes note of the cocktail's popularity in his volume of travel writing *Sketches and Travels in London* (1856).[20][21] It's not surprising that Scott and Thackeray, both fixtures in society who were deft at portraying contemporary social mores as well as historical moments, would include the drink du jour in their timely writings.

1 ½ ounces dry gin

¾ ounce lemon juice, freshly squeezed

½ ounce simple syrup (1 part sugar dissolved in 1 part water)

Lemon twist for garnishing

In a heatproof mug, combine gin, lemon juice, and simple syrup. Top with hot water and stir to combine. Garnish with the lemon twist.

1812 — 1870

Charles Dickens's
SHERRY COBBLER

SERVES 1

The prevailing style of Charles Dickens's Victorian England was one of abstention, teetotalism, and moral staunchness—but that didn't stop the author from indulging in spirits. In fact, both his fiction and his real life were punctuated by celebratory cocktails and frequent trips to the punch bowl.[22] When Dickens toured America, he marveled at the burgeoning cocktail scene, delighting in the gin slings, mint juleps, and timber doodles being whipped up behind the bar.[23] One of his favorites, the sherry cobbler, also makes a key appearance in his work. In *The Life and Adventures of Martin Chuzzlewit*, the titular character himself marvels at the drink, slurping it down in one eager sip.[24] Call us Victorian in our sensibilities, but we recommend a slower approach, savoring the interplay of fresh fruit with the salinity of the sherry.

2 orange slices

1 tablespoon sugar

4 ounces amontillado sherry

Berries (in season) for garnishing

Maraschino cherries for garnishing

1 lemon wheel for garnishing

Muddle orange slices and sugar at the bottom of a cocktail shaker. Add sherry and ice and shake. Strain ingredients into a collins glass filled with crushed ice. Garnish with seasonal berries, maraschino cherries, and a lemon wheel. Serve with a generosity of spirit. *Please sir,* your company will ask, *may I have another?*

1821 – – 1880

Gustave Flaubert's
FRENCH HOT TODDY*

SERVES 1

It follows that Gustave Flaubert's signature drink would be fragrant, sumptuous, and rich. He did, after all, not only make his famous antiheroine, Madame Bovary, a devotee of the sensuous world, but recognized his own behavior and tastes in hers. "Madame Bovary," he famously claimed, "*c'est moi*."[25] This French hot toddy, adapted from a recipe attributed to Flaubert in *The Alice B. Toklas Cook Book* (1954), delivers warm apple notes from cider and calvados, a French apple brandy, along with a supple layer of heavy cream—a drink that pairs well with an Emma Bovary-inspired afternoon of daydreams and romantic longing.

---

* Adapted from a recipe in *The Alice B. Toklas Cook Book*, 1954

| 4 ounces
apple cider | 2 ounces
apricot brandy | Ground
cinnamon for
garnishing |
| 2 ounces
calvados | 2 ounces
heavy cream | |

In a small saucepan, heat apple cider until warm. Remove from heat. Add calvados and apricot brandy, stirring to combine. Pour into a heatproof glass. Pouring in a circular motion, slowly add cream, allowing it to settle on top. Garnish with the cinnamon.

1828 — 1882

Dante Gabriel Rossetti's
CHLORAL WITH WHISKEY

SERVES 1

Whiskey, brandy, and laudanum however appear to have been administered more or less ad lib.[26] —"Some Medical Aspects of the Life of Dante Gabriel Rossetti," *Proceedings of the Royal Society of Medicine*, 1963

Chloral hydrate, a hypnotic drug, was discovered in the nineteenth century as a cure for insomnia; in application, it sometimes did the double duty of inducing paranoia and depression.[27] [28] Wash it down with a little whiskey, as famed Pre-Raphaelite painter and poet Dante Gabriel Rossetti was known to do, and you might feel the muse take hold—either that or waves of suspicion, reclusiveness, and social anxiety. Because we would hate to inspire these side effects in our dear readers, we implore you instead to replace the 10 grains of chloral (Rossetti's initial dose)[29] with 10 milligrams of CBD, or cannabidiol, a non-psychoactive, cannabis-based compound that has been popping up in craft cocktail bars and coffee shops all over the country. CBD, like chloral, can be used to treat insomnia and depression, and has been known to alleviate nausea, anxiety, and physical pain, without being habit-forming or hallucinatory.[30] One can only imagine that if the CBD boom had coincided with the Pre-Raphaelite heyday, Dante Gabriel Rossetti might have avoided a world of trouble.

10 milligrams
CBD tincture

2 ounces
whiskey

Combine CBD and whiskey in a rocks glass and enjoy.

FIVE O'CLOCK SOMEWHERE: LA CLOSERIE DES LILAS, THE BELLE EPOQUE, AND THE FLIGHT OF THE GREEN FAIRY

What difference is there between a glass of absinthe and a sunset?[31] —Oscar Wilde

WHO?

Charles Baudelaire, Paul-Marie Verlaine, Arthur Rimbaud, Colette, Oscar Wilde, Guillaume Apollinaire, and Alfred Jarry.

In the turn of the century, Paris, France, the late afternoon sun dapples the avenues and arrondissements. Around the city, especially here in Montparnasse, the intellectual elite stream into the counters and cafés lining the Left Bank. It is *l'heure verte*, or the green hour. The last brilliant bursts and fits of sunlight catch the pale-green poison and cast its hue across the mahogany bar of your favorite haunt, la Closerie des Lilas. You tip your glass to the familiar faces: Charles Baudelaire, Paul-Marie Verlaine, Arthur Rimbaud, Colette, Oscar Wilde, Guillaume Apollinaire, and Alfred Jarry.

Raucous and spirited hours spent debating philosophies, discussing literary works, and drinking absinthe on open-air terraces and in cozy booths gave the belle epoque of late-nineteenth- and early-twentieth-century Paris its trademark airs of mischief, rebellion, excess, and freedom. For every artfully prepared glass of absinthe, or the Green Fairy, there was a new idea, a new form, a new champion. Surrealists and poets took inspiration in the high-proof, peridot-hued aperitif flavored by wormwood, fennel, and anise, delighting in its hallucinatory claims; it was so popular at the time, in fact—thanks in part to its low cost compared to that of wine, which was in short supply due to disease-ravaged vineyards—that 5 p.m. was dubbed "the green hour," complete with a tell-tale licorice scent wafting through the streets.[32]

To properly enjoy absinthe, it is important to operate with a fidelity to tradition. The ritual of a drink, is, after all, part and

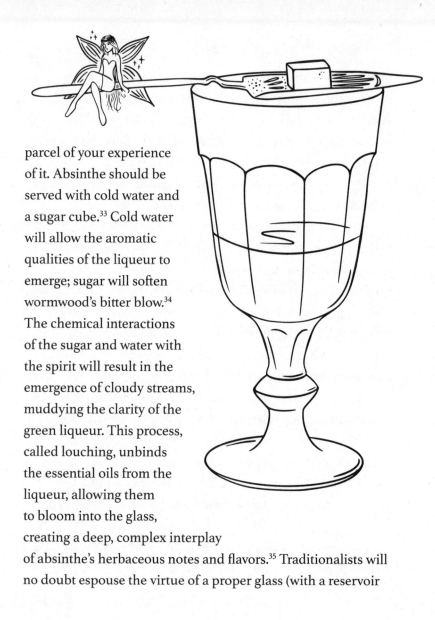

parcel of your experience
of it. Absinthe should be
served with cold water and
a sugar cube.[33] Cold water
will allow the aromatic
qualities of the liqueur to
emerge; sugar will soften
wormwood's bitter blow.[34]
The chemical interactions
of the sugar and water with
the spirit will result in the
emergence of cloudy streams,
muddying the clarity of the
green liqueur. This process,
called louching, unbinds
the essential oils from the
liqueur, allowing them
to bloom into the glass,
creating a deep, complex interplay
of absinthe's herbaceous notes and flavors.[35] Traditionalists will
no doubt espouse the virtue of a proper glass (with a reservoir

to indicate the correct volume of the drink) and a slotted spoon (to nestle the sugar cube over the mouth of the glass).[36]

That said, the great minds of turn-of-the-century Paris had their own methods—and resultant madness. The poet Alfred Jarry only drank his absinthe straight. Charles Baudelaire combined his with laudanum and opium. And Arthur Rimbaud paired the heady spirit with a bit of hashish.[37] Whichever way the writers greeted the Green Fairy, she found her way into their work. Baudelaire's famous poem "Be Drunk" was said to take its instructive title from the influence of absinthe; "The Poison," from his 1857 book *The Flowers of Evil*, places the intoxicating effects of absinthe over other drugs, namely wine and opium.[38]

Whether absinthe sparked the action of a short story, pushed a poet to pen ecstatic strophes, or inspired a painter's palette, it left indelible imprints on the artistic culture of the time and became a nostalgic touchstone for generations of writers to come. One in particular, Ernest Hemingway, crafted his own homage to the raucous, creative splendor of the belle epoque for a celebrity cocktail book published in the 1930s. Dubbed the Death in the Afternoon, the heady cocktail captures the essence of two distinct Parisian café cultures: l'heure verte of the turn of the century and the Lost Generation of the 1920s that followed.

1854 — 1900

Oscar Wilde's
ABSINTHE

SERVES 1

Three nights I sat up all night drinking absinthe, and thinking that I was singularly clearheaded and sane. The waiter came in and began watering the sawdust. The most wonderful flowers, tulips, lilies and roses sprang up and made a garden of the café. "Don't you see them," I said to him, "But Monsieur, there is nothing there."[39] —Oscar Wilde

| 1 ounce absinthe | 1 sugar cube |

Pour absinthe into absinthe glass. Place a slotted spoon over the mouth of the glass and set your sugar cube on top of it. Slowly drip 3 ounces ice water over the sugar cube, allowing the water to dissolve the sugar, dripping the sugar into the glass. Stir and enjoy.

1835 — 1910

Mark Twain's
WHISKY "COCK-TAIL"*

SERVES 1

S amuel Langhorne Clemens, also known as Mark Twain, was an early adopter of cocktails as we know them today. When he returned to the States from a tour of speaking engagements in London, he brought back with him an appreciation for Scotch whisky complemented by citrus and sugar. He felt that the mixture aided his digestion, and also gave him an amorous push. He implored his wife to have the cocktail waiting for him at home, promising her a bevy of kisses in return.[40]

---

* Adapted from a letter Twain wrote to his wife dated January 1874

Livy my darling, I want you to be sure and remember to have, in the bathroom, when I arrive, a bottle of Scotch whisky, a lemon, some crushed sugar, and a bottle of Angostura bitters. Ever since I have been in London I have taken in a wine glass what is called a cock-tail (made with those ingredients) before breakfast, before dinner, and just before going to bed.[41]

—Mark Twain in letter to wife Olivia Langdon Clemens, 1874

2 ounces
Scotch whisky

½ ounce lemon juice,
freshly squeezed

½ ounce
simple syrup
(1 part sugar dissolved
in 1 part water)

2 dashes
angostura bitters
for garnishing

Combine whisky, lemon juice, and simple syrup in a cocktail shaker filled with ice. Shake to blend, strain into a chilled coupe glass, and garnish with bitters. Enjoy cock-tail "before breakfast, before dinner, and just before going to bed."[42]

1865 — — 1939

William Butler Yeats's
CLOVER CLUB*

 SERVES 1

The Clover Club cocktail, named for a group of lawyers, bankers, and powerful men who gathered at the Bellevue-Stratford Hotel in the late 1880s, originated in Philadelphia but found its way onto ritzy menus all over the East Coast in the early twentieth century.[43] Irish poet William Butler Yeats was said to be so enamored with this slightly sweet, slightly sour pink cocktail that he drank three in a row during a visit to New York.[44]

---

* Recipe from Julie Reiner, proprietor of the Clover Club in Brooklyn, New York

Wine comes in at the mouth
And love comes in at the eye
That's all we shall know for truth
Before we grow old and die.
I lift the glass to my mouth
I look at you, and I sigh.[45]

—"A Drinking Song," 1915

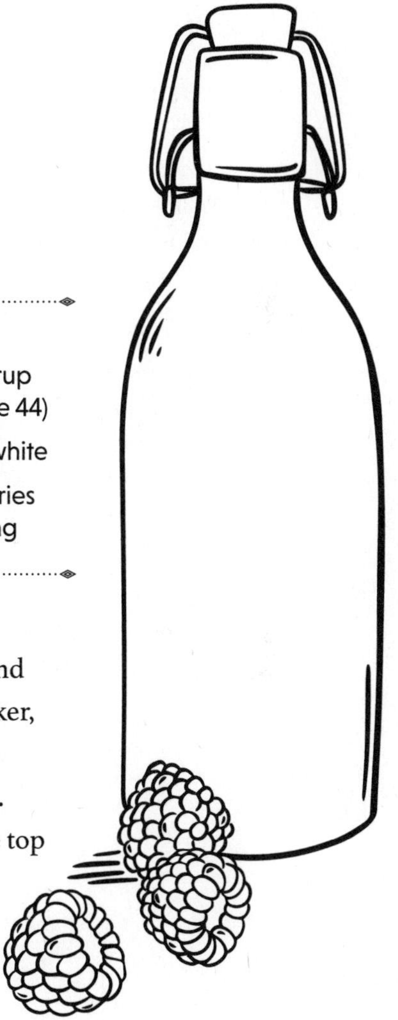

1 ½ ounces gin

½ ounce dry
vermouth

½ ounce
lemon juice,
freshly squeezed

½ ounce
Raspberry Syrup
(see recipe page 44)

¼ ounce egg white

2 or 3 raspberries
for garnishing

Combine all ingredients in a cocktail
shaker with ice, shake until chilled, and
strain. Return mix to the cocktail shaker,
this time without ice, and shake until
frothy. Pour into a chilled coupe glass.
Skewer raspberries and lay across the top
of the drink to garnish.

Raspberry Syrup

½ cup fresh
raspberries

1 cup sugar
½ ounce vodka

Muddle raspberries with sugar and let sit for 20 to 30 minutes. Warm ½ cup water and pour over muddled berries, stirring until sugar has dissolved. Strain into a glass bottle or jar through a chinois or a cheesecloth, and add vodka to the liquid. The vodka acts as a preservative in the syrup, which keeps in the refrigerator for one month.

F. Scott Fitzgerald's
GIN RICKEY

SERVES 1

"First you take a drink," goes F. Scott Fitzgerald's frequently recited distillation of inebriation, "then the drink takes a drink, then the drink takes you."[46] The life and works of the beloved author are steeped in booze. *The Great Gatsby*, sopped by champagne and its trademark sparkle, leaves as an aftertaste the burning solemnity of a gin martini. When he was off the wagon, Fitzgerald liked gin best (he thought it was hard for others to detect it on his breath).[47] When he was drying out, he stuck to beer, which he drank like water.[48]

2 ounces gin	Soda water
¾ ounce lime juice, freshly squeezed	Lime wheel for garnishing

Fill a collins glass with ice. Add gin and lime juice, and top with soda water. Garnish with the lime wheel. Dance naked in a fountain with your favorite southern belle.

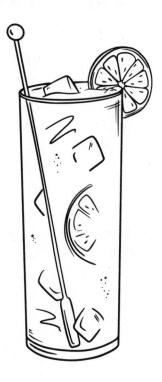

1882 — 1941

James Joyce's
DUBLIN COFFEE

SERVES 1

The light music of whiskey falling into a glass made an agreeable interlude.[49] —*Dubliners*, 1914

What could be more quintessentially Irish than James Joyce and a Dublin coffee? This recipe, adapted from *The Alice B. Toklas Cook Book* (1954), would have kept the coffee-loving writer of *Finnegans Wake*, *Ulysses*, and *Dubliners* warm on characteristically rainy, overcast Dublin days.[50]

2 ounces Irish whiskey	1 teaspoon sugar 4 ounces hot coffee	1 ounce heavy cream

In a heatproof balloon wine glass (a wine glass with a bulbous shape), combine Irish whiskey and sugar. Pour in coffee, and stir slowly. While stirring, slowly add cream in a circular motion. Let the cream settle on top; do not stir again.

Aphra Behn
and Virginia Woolf's
MILK PUNCH*

SERVES 30

Punch! 'Tis my Morning's Draught, my Table-drink, my Treat, my Regalia, my everything.[51] —Aphra Behn, *The Widow Ranter*, 1688

Oftentimes, writers look to the past for guidance and inspiration. They take up the threads of old traditions and fold them into new tapestries. They engage in conversation with those who came before them, particularly those brave artists who cleared paths for new voices and styles in their own generations. Virginia Woolf, author of *The Hours* and *Mrs.*

---

* Adapted from *How to Mix Drinks: Or, The Bon-Vivant's Companion* by Jerry Thomas, 1862

Above left: Aphra Behn
Above right: Virginia Woolf

Dalloway, held a special appreciation for Aphra Behn, a playwright, poet, and translator who, in seventeenth-century England, became one of the first women to earn a living through writing. As Woolf once said of Behn, "it was she who earned [women] the right to speak their minds."[52] Behn was an innovative and influential force in Restoration-era England; a sexually empowered literary mind who knew her way around palace intrigue and entertaining.[53] She is widely credited as the mind behind milk punch, a captivating drink created by mixing, steeping, and then straining a combination of full-fat milk, alcohol, citrus, and aromatics like tea, herbs, and spices.[54]

This clarified punch grew in popularity in England, and with colonists like Benjamin Franklin, throughout the eighteenth century and beyond.[55] One proponent of the complex, crowd-pleasing tipple? Leslie Stephen, father of Virginia Woolf.[56] It would surprise us little if Woolf herself didn't occasionally indulge in milk punch; after all, she was a key member of London's Bloomsbury Group, a small circle of artists, writers, and friends who were known to enjoy one another's company and traditional English treats over long suppers, luncheons, and weekends in the country.[57] Clarified milk punch, a classic at parties and special occasions, would not have been out of place on the menu.

While the name "milk punch" evokes the creamy, dessert-like quality of eggnog, this elegant drink relies on milk for its scientific properties rather than its richness. When milk is added to the base of the punch, it curdles.[58] When the curds are strained, a crystal-clear liquid with a soft, subtle flavor will emerge.[59] If stored in a cool place, it can keep for months or even years.[60]

To make a clarified milk punch, you will need cheesecloth or a chinois, patience, and thirty friends to share with. For the chemical process of clarification to occur, you must use full-fat milk. If you are avoiding dairy, full-fat coconut milk makes a nice substitution.

6 lemons	20 coriander seeds	1 cup Puerto Rican rum
1 pound sugar	1 star anise	
1 pineapple, peeled, cored, and cut into 1-inch cubes	2 cups cognac	1 cup brewed green tea
	1 cup light Jamaican rum	⅔ cup Batavia Arrack
6 cloves	1 cup overproof Jamaican rum	4 cups whole milk
1 cinnamon stick		

In a very large heat-safe pitcher, combine the juice of 4 of the lemons and the zest of 2. Add the sugar, pineapple, cloves, cinnamon, coriander, star anise, cognac, rum, green tea, and Batavia Arrack, then add 2 cups boiling water. Cover and steep at room temperature for at least 6 hours.

Warm milk in a saucepan. Once hot, add it to the punch mixture in the pitcher. Add the juice of the remaining 2 lemons and stir to mix. The milk will curdle and solids will form. Let mixture sit for 30 minutes, then strain through a chinois or a fine strainer lined with cheesecloth. Strain once more to clear out any remaining cloudiness. Transfer to clean bottles and store at cool room temperature. Serve over ice.

Alexander Woollcott's
WHILE ROME BURNS COCKTAIL*

 SERVES 1

All the things I really like to do are either immoral, illegal, or fattening.[61] —*"The Knock at the Stage Door,"* 1933

Alexander Woollcott was a legendary wit, drama critic, and self-appointed leader of the Algonquin Round Table. His specialty cocktail, which he crafted for a 1935 collection of celebrity recipes, combines the smack of lemon, the sweet hint of maple syrup, and the rich, molasses notes

---

* From *So Red the Nose or—Breath in the Afternoon,* 1935

of Medford Rum.[62] The result is a delightfully sharp and a pleasantly plump sip—one that recalls the smart aleck himself.

| 2 ounces Medford Rum | 1 ounce lemon juice, freshly squeezed | 1 dash maple syrup |

Combine all ingredients in a cocktail shaker with ice. Shake until well chilled. Pour into a chilled coupe glass straight up, or into a rocks glass over ice.

NOTE: Medford Rum was originally produced in New England in the early eighteenth century, but production came to a halt at the start of the twentieth century due to the rising cost of molasses (a key ingredient in rum) as well as the blow of Prohibition. In recent years, several distillers have taken up the traditional method with hopes of bringing Medford Rum back to its prior glory.[63]

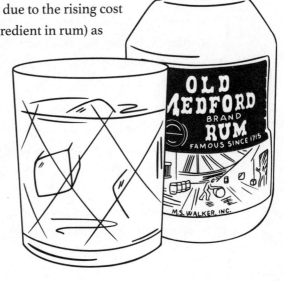

1884 – 1945

William Seabrook's
ASYLUM COCKTAIL*

 SERVES 1

Travel writer, occultist, cannibal, and journalist William Buehler Seabrook was obsessed with a mysticism of darkness—preoccupied in part by pain, sadism, and the undead.[64] In fact, he popularized the term "zombie" in the West and was fixated on the art of voodoo.[65] He also spent plenty of time institutionalized, a fact that is crystallized in the name of this drink. Seabrook claims that this heady libation will "look like rosy dawn, taste like the milk of Paradise, and make you plenty crazy."[66]

---

* From *So Red the Nose or—Breath in the Afternoon*, 1935

1 ½ ounces gin

1 ½ ounces Pernod

1 dash grenadine
(see recipe page 103)

Combine all ingredients in a large mixing glass, add ice, and stir until chilled. Pour into a rocks glass over "large lumps" of ice.[67]

1900 — 1948

Zelda Fitzgerald's
VODKA LEMONADE

SERVES 1

Zelda Sayre Fitzgerald lived according to the ethos spelled out so clearly on her senior yearbook page: "Why should all life be work, when we all can borrow? / Let's think only of today, and not worry about tomorrow."[68] She was ebullient and incandescent, at mercy to the ecstasies and travails that come with being radically present. With her husband, F. Scott Fitzgerald, she embarked on a life of high romance, destruction, and exuberant obsession.[69] She was a devoted dancer, a playful fixture on the party circuit, and a brilliant writer—so brilliant, in fact, that F. Scott Fitzgerald cribbed her letters and witticisms to fortify his own novels.[70] The pair shared more than a love for each other and each other's words; they fostered an abiding affection for the bottle. F. Scott was a gin drinker, but Zelda Sayre, true to her roots as a southern belle, preferred her refreshment in the form of a vodka lemonade—the consummate companion to a sprawling porch and a day spent socializing.[71]

1 ½ ounces vodka

3 ounces lemonade

Lavender sprig
for garnishing

In a collins glass, combine vodka with ice, then top with lemonade. Stir to combine. Garnish with the lavender sprig.

George Orwell's
NICE CUP OF TEA

SERVES 1

George Orwell took a measured view of alcohol and the
culture that surrounded it. A fan of its potential as a social
good that could unite families and friends in neighborhood
pubs and gathering places, Orwell was keenly aware of a drink's
ability to foster congeniality, familiarity, and comfort. He was
also aware of its ruinous potential. "A man may take to drink
because he feels himself a failure," Orwell wrote, "but then fail
all the more because he drinks."[72]

Orwell himself was a beer drinker who longed for a
pint of Simpson's dark mild and the perfect pub—quiet
enough to hold a conversation, spacious and clean enough to

accommodate families, and staffed by warm bartenders who never forgot a patron's name.[73] There would be a roaring fire, a garden in the back, and a menu of light snacks. He named this fictive pub, this beacon in his mind's eye, "The Moon Under Water" in a 1946 essay.[74]

Orwell encountered the predicament of a cup of tea—which, unlike his alcohol, he wanted full-strength—with the same sense of specificity and idealism that he brought to the public house.

GEORGE ORWELL'S TIPS FOR TEA*

1. One should always use Indian or Ceylon tea. While Chinese tea has beneficial qualities, it will not offer the vigorous physical and mental stimulation that Indian and Ceylon teas provide.

2. Quality over quantity; use a small teapot—no industrial urns.

3. Prior to use, warm the teapot by placing it near the stove.

4. The stronger the tea, the better. For every quart of hot water, use 6 teaspoons of tea.

5. Refuse strainers or teabags; the tea should be steeped directly in the pot.

---

* Adapted from "A Nice Cup of Tea," 1946

6. The hotter the water, the better. Keep the teapot right next to the kettle. The water should be at its very hottest the moment it meets the tea. Every moment counts.

7. After adding the hot water to the teapot, give it a good shake to agitate the tea leaves before they settle.

8. Drink the tea out of a sturdy, cylindrical breakfast mug. No dainty teacups here.

9. Skim any cream off of the milk. According to Orwell, milk that is too creamy "always gives tea a sickly taste."[75]

10. Pour the tea into the cup before adding the milk.

11. No sugar. "Tea is meant to be bitter," writes Orwell, "just as beer is meant to be bitter."[76]

Edgar Rice Burroughs's
TARZAN COCKTAIL*

 **SERVES 1**

*T*arzan of the Apes author Edgar Rice Burroughs designed this cocktail with the tropics in mind. Have a few sips and you'll be king of the jungle in no time.

1 ounce rum

1 teaspoon Cointreau

½ ounce lime juice, freshly squeezed

½ ounce simple syrup (1 part sugar dissolved in 1 part water)

Lime wheel for garnishing

---

* From *So Red the Nose or—Breath in the Afternoon,* 1935

Combine rum, Cointreau, lime juice, and simple syrup in a cocktail shaker with ice and shake until chilled. Strain into a chilled coupe glass, and garnish with the lime wheel.

Edna St. Vincent Millay's
BETWEEN THE
SHEETS

SERVES 1

T he Pulitzer Prize–winning confessional poet was known to imbibe this variation of the classic sidecar while slinging drinks behind the bar at Chumley's, an iconic speakeasy in the West Village of Manhattan that saw the likes of John Steinbeck, Simone de Beauvoir, F. Scott Fitzgerald, and a cross section of influential Beat poets who drank, loved, and napped in its dimly lit, subterranean digs.[77]

1 ounce brandy

1 ounce light rum

1 ounce triple sec

½ ounce
lemon juice,
freshly squeezed

Lemon twist
for garnishing

Combine brandy, light rum, triple sec, and lemon juice in a cocktail shaker with ice. Shake vigorously. Strain into a chilled coupe glass and garnish with the lemon twist. Serve at your writing workshop's next speakeasy theme night, or just drink it alone in your basement with the lights off.

Eugene O'Neill's
GIBSON

SERVES 1

Celebrated widely as America's Shakespeare, Nobel laureate Eugene O'Neill approached his drinking as he did his writing: with a heightened awareness of family tension, torturous commitment, and an air of the dramatic.[78] O'Neill hailed from a family of roving addicts and alcoholics; his father, in particular, foisted upon him the difficult birthright of drinking to excess, visiting sex workers, and generally raising hell.[79] He was even booted from Princeton University for chucking a bottle through the university president's window after one particularly raucous evening. (That president? Woodrow Wilson.[80]) Through psychoanalysis, the dramatist who penned *Long Day's Journey into Night*, *The Iceman*

Cometh, and *Anna Christie* eventually bested his familial influence and subsequent abuse of alcohol. But before he did, O'Neill was known to linger over cocktails at New York dive bars.[81] And the Gibson, smacking of brine, salinity, and the cool promise of forgetting, was rumored to be his drink of choice.[82]

2 ounces gin ½ ounce dry vermouth	¼ ounce brine from cocktail onion jar	3 cocktail pearl onions for garnishing

In a large mixing glass combine gin, vermouth, and brine. Add ice and stir until well chilled. Strain into a chilled coupe glass. Garnish with the cocktail onions.

1888 — 1959

Raymond Chandler's
GIMLET

SERVES 1

There's no question that gimlets were Raymond Chandler's favorite drink. The gin cocktail took a star-making turn in Chandler's penultimate detective novel *The Long Goodbye*, where it is mentioned twenty-one times throughout the pages.[83] Introduced to the private investigator Philip Marlowe by Terry Lennox, the gimlet arrives with an air of authoritative specificity. "A real gimlet is half gin and half Rose's Lime Juice and nothing else," Lennox explains to Marlowe. "It beats martinis hollow."[84] To make the cocktail palatable for modern drinkers (while rumor has it Rose's Lime Juice used to be made with real sugar, today the concoction smacks of corn syrup[85]), we've altered the ratio and introduced a bit of fresh lime. Hopefully Lennox will forgive the transgression—or at least forget it by the time the bottle of Beefeater runs dry.

2 ounces gin

½ ounce Rose's Lime Juice

½ ounce lime juice, freshly squeezed

Lime slice for garnishing

Combine gin, Rose's Lime Juice, and fresh lime juice in a cocktail shaker filled with ice. Shake vigorously. Strain into a chilled coupe glass. Garnish with the lime slice.

1894 — 1961

Dashiell Hammett's
THE THIN MANHATTAN

SERVES 1

Dashiell Hammett's Prohibition-era detective novels bear the influences of his surroundings. While he was writing noir classics like *The Thin Man* and *The Maltese Falcon*, he lived in San Francisco's Tenderloin, a crime-ridden neighborhood studded with speakeasies and bootleggers.[86] The Manhattan may belong to the East Coast in name, but it complements the Northern California city—the warm, pepper-forward notes from the rye

cutting through the cloak of mist and fog.[87] The Manhattan transcends the lines of fiction and composition: this boozy, stirred classic is at home in the grasp of a seasoned detective or nestled by the ashtray and typewriter of the troubled author who conjures his spirit.

2 ounces rye whiskey

1 ounce sweet vermouth

2 dashes angostura bitters

Luxardo cherry for garnishing

In a mixing glass, combine rye, vermouth, and angostura bitters. Add ice and stir, combining ingredients, until well chilled. Strain into a chilled coupe glass and garnish with the Luxardo cherry.

1899 — — 1961

Ernest Hemingway's
LOCAL LIBATIONS

SERVES 1

Reading Hemingway feels, at times, like ponying up to a Key West dive; at others, like biding your time at a mahogany counter in a European capital, waiting for your lover to arrive. In nearly every story, cocktails accompany emotionally fraught scenes, crystallizing character development and pushing the plot forward. Hemingway's spare prose leaves no room for set decoration; rather, he deploys the concrete world, alcohol included, in service of his stories' emotional force.

The saying, "write what you know" has never applied more faithfully to a writer than it does to Hemingway, who managed to become a regular at a handful of bars around the world, and even developed his own iconic cocktails.[88] He drank often and amply, but "Papa," as he was called, remained beloved by barkeeps and proprietors for his cheery disposition and loyal patronage.[89] Whether it was absinthe on the Left Bank of Paris, beers in Madrid, or rum in the tropics, Hemingway appreciated local libations and made himself at home in the bars, pubs, cafés, and beer halls punctuating the old cities and sandy beaches that claimed him in return.[90]

PAPA DOBLE DAIQUIRI (AT EL FLORIDITA)

As legend holds, Hemingway chanced into Havana, Cuba's El Floridita, caught the bartender serving up frozen drinks, tried them, and declared, "that's good but I'd prefer it without the sugar . . . and double the rum."[91] While Hemingway loathed sweet drinks and allegedly preferred a scant six drops of maraschino liqueur in his daiquiri to complement his rum, most modern bartenders up the amount for a more palatable sip.[92]

2 ounces light rum	½ ounce grapefruit juice, freshly squeezed	¼ ounce maraschino liqueur
¾ ounce lime juice, freshly squeezed		Lime wheel for garnishing

Combine rum, lime juice, grapefruit juice, and maraschino liqueur in a cocktail shaker filled with ice and shake vigorously until chilled. Strain into a chilled coupe glass. Garnish with the lime wheel.

Mojito (at La Bodeguita del Medio?)[93]

There is an inscription on the wall at La Bodeguita del Medio in Havana, Cuba, in Hemingway's handwriting: "My mojito in La Bodeguita, my daquiri in El Floridita." But, according to cocktail historian Philip Greene, this inscription might be a fake; while record indeed shows Papa swilling countless daquiris at the Floridita bar, there's no definitive proof that Hemingway drank mojitos at La Bodeguita.[94] Still, Greene writes that Hemingway did in fact enjoy a cocktail that resembled a classic mojito, prepared by Gregario, the skipper of his beloved boat, Pilar.[95]

1 ½ ounces light rum

1 ounce honey syrup (1 part honey dissolved in 1 part water)

1 ounce lime juice, freshly squeezed

4 mint leaves

Splash club soda

Lime wedge for garnishing

Combine rum, honey syrup, lime juice, and mint leaves in a cocktail shaker filled with ice and shake vigorously until chilled. Pour into a collins glass over ice and top with club soda. Garnish with the lime wedge.

DEATH IN THE AFTERNOON

1 ½ ounces absinthe   Champagne

Pour absinthe into a champagne flute. Top with champagne
until the drink "attains a proper opalescent milkiness."[96]
Hemingway recommends drinking three to five of these
cocktails, slowly.

Right: A young Ernest Hemingway

William Faulkner's
MINT JULEP

 SERVES 1

Born and raised in the Deep South, William Faulkner was notoriously devoted to corn whiskey. When Sherwood Anderson met the author of *Light in August* and *The Sound and the Fury* in New Orleans, he was wearing an overcoat stuffed with jars of moonshine.[97] On cold nights, Faulkner would reach for a hot toddy, but nothing paired better with the Mississippi swelter than a simple, classic mint julep—prepared, of course, in a frosty metal cup.[98]

| 1 or 2 mint sprigs | 1 teaspoon cane sugar | 2 ounces bourbon (to start) |

At the bottom of a chilled julep cup, muddle mint sprigs with sugar and a splash of cold water (preferably rainwater, distilled, from a cistern) using a cocktail muddler or the blunt end of a wooden spoon. Fill cup with crushed ice and pour bourbon over, liberally.

1925 — 1964

Flannery O'Connor's
COCA-COLA PLUS

SERVES 1

In her too-short thirty-nine years on earth, Flannery O'Connor made an indelible mark on American literature. Though she published only two novels and nineteen stories before she died from complications related to lupus, O'Connor is largely regarded as a master of the short story form; she cemented a memorable reputation as an enthusiastic proponent of Catholicism, the ironic voice of the rural South, and an eccentric, darkly comic figure who once gifted her mother a mule and was known to enjoy Coca-Cola mixed with coffee.[99] [100]

2 ounces coffee, room temperature or cooler	1 ½ ounces spiced rum 2 ounces Coca-Cola	Lemon wedge for garnishing

Combine coffee and rum in a collins glass. Add ice.
Top with Coca-Cola and garnish with the lemon wedge.

1908 — 1964

Ian Fleming's
VESPER MARTINI

SERVES 1

James Bond, the iconic international man-of-mystery-cum-lady-killer who first came to life in Ian Fleming's 1953 novel *Casino Royale*, invites admiration and imitation. Suave, cunning, dapper, Bond abides by a high standard of style. He really only commits one faux pas: ordering his martinis shaken, not stirred. Shaking the cocktail upsets the aromatic quality of the liquor—studies have even shown that agitating the delicate spirits might result in the significant loss of gin's prized botanical flavor.[101] Besides, shaking welcomes the addition of ice chips into the drink, needlessly complicating the smooth and clean sip of a proper martini.

Fleming created the Vesper for his protagonist. Like 007 himself, this martini variation is strong, timeless, creative, and classic. If, like Bond, you have important business to conduct after hours, limit yourself to one Vesper and make it count: "I never have more than one drink before dinner. But I do like that one to be large and very strong and very cold and very well-made. I hate small portions of anything, especially when they taste bad."[102]

"A dry martini," he said. "One. In a deep champagne goblet. . . . Just a moment. Three measures of Gordon's, one of vodka, half a measure of Kina Lillet. Shake it very well until it's ice-cold, then add a large thin slice of lemon-peel. Got it?"[103] —*Casino Royale*, 1953

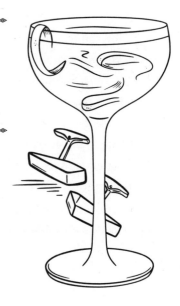

3 ounces gin (Gordon's Dry)
1 ounce vodka
½ ounce Lillet Blanc
Lemon peel for garnishing

In a large mixing glass filled with ice, combine gin, vodka, and Lillet. Stir until sufficiently chilled. Strain into a deep champagne goblet. Garnish with the lemon peel.

1874 — 1965

Somerset Maugham's
ŻUBRÓWKA

SERVES 1

This vodka, infused with bison grass, carries notes of lavender, vanilla, and cut grass.[104] In his 1944 novel *The Razor's Edge*, Somerset Maugham wrote that the Polish delicacy "smells of freshly mowed hay and spring flowers, of thyme and lavender, and it's soft on the palate and so comfortable, it's like listening to music by moonlight."[105] Thinly veiled as the novel was understood to be,[106] it's fair to surmise that this affection for the liquor was Maugham's own. Prepared simply over ice with apple juice—a pairing as traditional as gin and tonic—the herbaceous, ethereal spirit sings.

| 2 ounces Żubrówka (Polish bison grass vodka) | 4 ounces apple juice, freshly pressed | Lime wedge for garnishing |

Pour Żubrówka into a collins glass. Add ice. Top with apple juice and garnish with the lime wedge.

1903 — 1966

Evelyn Waugh's
STINGER

SERVES 1

S weet and fresh, the stinger is a cocktail that you'll want to [*Brideshead*] revisit[*ed*] time and time again. Be forewarned: innocent though it may taste given its peppermint essence, this drink has seen the *Decline and Fall* of many great minds, Waugh's included. The satirical novelist developed such an affection for crème de menthe that he even mixed it with the bromide he was prescribed to quell his aches and insomnia—and suffered a deep psychosis thereafter.[107]

1 sprig mint	2 ounces brandy	Mint leaf for garnishing
¾ ounce crème de menthe	½ ounce dry vermouth	

In a cocktail shaker, muddle mint with crème de menthe. Add brandy, dry vermouth, and ice and shake to combine. Strain into a chilled martini glass, or enjoy in a rocks glass over ice. Garnish with the mint leaf.

1926 — 1966

Frank O'Hara's
STREGA AND COKE

SERVES 1

O ne of the most distinguished members of the New
York School of poets, Frank O'Hara crafted a lively
style of verse imbued with the quotidian, the personal, and
the ecstatic—at once jarringly present in feeling and mired
in his cultural moment. Just like O'Hara's poetry, which
bounces breathlessly between highbrow art and pop culture,
this cocktail combined the herbaceous, esoteric elegance
of Liquore Strega, an Italian digestif with coniferous notes,
with the ubiquitous flavor of Coca-Cola, an American
favorite and a staple in every household. The eclectic
nature of the combination makes for a cocktail nearly

as compelling, cheeky, and compulsively consumable as O'Hara's verse itself.

1 ½ ounces Liquore Strega	4 ounces Coca-Cola	Lemon twist for garnishing

Pour Strega into a collins or highball glass. Fill glass with ice and top with Coke. Garnish with the lemon twist.

1874–1946   1877–1967

Gertrude Stein and Alice B. Toklas's
SUMMER CHAMPAGNE FRUIT SALAD*

SERVES 1

It is fitting that Stein, with her staunch appetite, was a good match for Alice B. Toklas, who took to crafting recipes with the same delight as Stein took to testing the results.[108] At their home in Paris, Stein and Toklas hosted a revolving-door cast of poets, painters, and intellectuals.[109] While Stein meted out art criticism and argued the finer points of surrealism in the Picasso-studded rooms of 27 rue de Fleurus, Toklas

---

* Adapted from *The Alice B. Toklas Cook Book*, 1954

Above left: Gertrude Stein
Above right: Alice B. Toklas

experimented in the kitchen to great avail. Her recipes, like one for Hashish Fudge, exuded both playfulness and attention to detail—qualities that were in kind with the poetics and artistry of those whom she served.[110]

Eating is her subject.[111] —Gertrude Stein, "Christian Bérard," 1934

1 large, ripe cantaloupe	½ cup sliced peaches	¾ cup very dry champagne
½ cup pineapple, cubed	1 cup raspberries	2 tablespoons kirsch
	1 tablespoon fine sugar, or to taste	2 tablespoons white crème de menthe

Cut an opening on one end of the melon and scoop out the seeds, keeping the lopped-off end. Add the other fruits and sugar if needed. Pour champagne, kirsch, and crème de menthe over the fruit. Place the reserved end back on top of the melon and chill, standing, overnight in the refrigerator. Serve with more champagne to your nearest and dearest surrealists.

Dorothy Parker's
WHISKEY SOUR

 SERVES 1

Enjoy this cocktail midday and delight in dazzling your most illustrious colleagues. Do take heed—there's a difference between wit and wisecracking. To keep your one-liners pithy and your couplets rhyming, remember the rule of thumb frequently attributed to Ms. Parker (though suspiciously absent from her poems and books):[112]

> I love a martini
> But two at the very most.
> Three, I'm under the table.
> Four, I'm under the host.

2 ounces bourbon

¾ ounce
lemon juice

¾ ounce simple
syrup (1 part
sugar dissolved
in 1 part water)

Lemon peel and
a maraschino cherry,
for garnishing

Combine bourbon, lemon juice, and simple syrup in a cocktail
shaker filled with ice. Shake vigorously to combine. Strain into
a chilled coupe glass and garnish with
the lemon peel and a cherry.

THE ALGONQUIN
ROUND TABLE

WHO?

A dozen or so writers, editors, and critics; namely, Dorothy
Parker, Harold Ross, Robert Benchley, Franklin Pierce Adams,
Heywood Broun, Alexander Woollcott, George S. Kaufman,
Ruth Hale, Edna Ferber, and Robert Sherwood.[113]

WHAT?

The Algonquin Round Table refers to more than just
a gathering place. It was an idea, an era, a mood, and,
sometimes, a performance. The Round Table crew—dubbed
the "Vicious Circle," united by their acerbic wit and sharp
tongues, and bolstered by the buoyant artistic energy that
defined the period after World War I—gathered each day at
lunchtime, delighting in verbal jousts, lighthearted barbs,
cultural criticism, and perfectly crafted whiskey sours. They
collaborated with one another, commissioned columns and

pieces of criticism from other members of the group, and enlivened the New York literary scene as a whole through a shared discernment.[114]

WHERE?

The Algonquin Hotel, on 44th Street and 6th Avenue in midtown Manhattan, conveniently located near the offices of the *New Yorker*, Harold Ross's burgeoning magazine, which employed several Round Table members as critics and columnists. The group first met at the long table in the Pergola Room and eventually moved to the Rose Room to accommodate its swelling size and the crowds that sometimes gathered to observe the exchange of barbs and ideas.[115]

WHEN?

The literary Who's Who first gathered for lunch at the hotel in 1919, and continued sharing jibes, notes, gossip, and cocktails every day thereafter, sparking a literary renaissance in the heart of midtown. The spirit of the thirties, dampened by the Great Depression and darkening geo-political forces, saw a loosening of the group's once tight-knit bonds. The Round Table crew met for the final time in 1943.[116]

What Were They Drinking?

The heyday of the Round Table coincided with Prohibition, but that couldn't stop the group of artists and writers from indulging in their favorite spirits.

Martinis, of course, were on the docket, though a house cocktail, too, emerged from the Algonquin, and the recipe lives on courtesy of cocktail historian David Wondrich.[117]

The Algonquin

1 ½ ounces rye whiskey

¾ ounce blanc vermouth

¾ ounce pineapple juice

¼ ounce honey syrup
(2 parts honey dissolved
in 1 part hot water)

Combine rye, vermouth, pineapple juice, and honey syrup in a cocktail shaker filled with ice. Shake vigorously to combine and strain into a chilled coupe glass.

1917 — 1967

Carson McCullers's
"SONNIE BOY"

 SERVES 1

C arson McCullers mourned that she had arrived at the end
of the end of something. As bombs struck Britain and the
Second World War swept Europe, McCullers looked wistfully at
the Paris of the 1920s, at the literary circles and artistic conviviality
that she would never be a part of. She, too, wanted her cultural
movement, and with her group of friends, including W. H.
Auden, Gypsy Rose Lee, and George Davis, decided to craft one.[118]
They moved into a brownstone on Middagh Street in Brooklyn
Heights; there, as dishes stacked up in the sink and cold wind
drafted through gaps in the window frames, the group of friends
shared meals, notes on their writing, and occasionally beds. The

menagerie survived on stories, camaraderie, and little else; Auden rationed their toilet paper, and water ran cold through the winter. McCullers was known to spend her paltry earnings on jugs of sherry.[119] The author of *The Heart is a Lonely Hunter* would mix it with tea and lemon and keep it by her side at all times, kept warm in a thermos she'd nicknamed "Sonnie Boy."[120]

⅔ cup hot tea

⅓ cup dry sherry
(amontillado is ideal,
but any sherry
in a pinch is fine)

Squeeze lemon juice

Boil water and steep tea for 2 or 3 minutes before stirring in sherry. Finish with a big squeeze of lemon. Serve in a thermos and—this is important—drink all day. If you have some pages to crank out, a strong, caffeinated English breakfast tea will serve you well.

NOTE: Pairs well with McCullers's favorite "Spuds Carson," a dish of creamed potatoes, ripe olives, minced onion, and grated cheese.[121]

1902 — 1968

John Steinbeck's
JACK ROSE

SERVES 1

Steinbeck's great American novels *The Grapes of Wrath, East of Eden,* and *Of Mice and Men* revealed the bitter truth of economic hardship. His ability to render the human condition with sympathy, humor, and realism gained him the Nobel Prize for Literature in 1962.[122] The enormity of his artistic and social task—to convey the daily travails of rural laborers, tenant farmers, and the American family with tenderness, grit, and imagination—was matched by the size of his appetite for a good, stiff cocktail.[123] Enter the Jack Rose, a classic in its day that was also adored by Ernest Hemingway, who makes mention of the brandy-based drink in *The Sun Also Rises*.[124]

2 ounces Laird's applejack	½ ounce lemon juice, freshly squeezed	½ ounce lime juice, freshly squeezed
½ ounce grenadine (recipe below)		Lemon peel for garnishing

Combine applejack, grenadine, lemon juice, and lime juice in a cocktail shaker filled with ice. Shake well and strain into a chilled coupe glass. Garnish with the lemon peel.

GRENADINE*

1 quart pomegranate juice

½ pound demerara sugar

1 tablespoon rose water

1 tablespoon orange-blossom water

In a small saucepan, combine all ingredients and heat over medium, stirring, until sugar dissolves. Store in the fridge for up to 1 week.

---

* Adapted from the *New York Times*

1922 — 1969

Jack Kerouac's
MARGARITA

 SERVES 1

Jack Kerouac, author of *The Dharma Bums* and *On the Road*, embraced spontaneity in his prose, seeking to convey an authentic immediacy in his novels and pushing the mantra "first thought, best thought" where prose was concerned.[125] During one of his many sojourns to Mexico, he found the drink that aligned with his spirit: stimulating, honest, easy to binge.[126] It was the classic margarita, a simple and lively cocktail that tastes best in its purest form—without tinkering, without complication, without revision.

2 ounces silver tequila	¾ ounce lime juice, freshly squeezed	Rock salt for garnishing
¾ ounce Cointreau	1 teaspoon agave nectar (optional)	Lime wedge for garnishing

Pour salt onto a small plate. Rub a lime wedge around the lip of a rocks glass and dip the rim in the salt. In a cocktail shaker filled with ice, combine tequila, Cointreau, lime juice, and agave, if using. Shake vigorously. Strain into the salt-rimmed rocks glass over ice. Garnish with the lime wedge.

PAIR WITH: tortilla chips, guacamole, and Benzedrine (we kid).

VESUVIO CAFÉ

WHO?

Vesuvio Café catered to a crowd of beatniks—a group of Benzedrine-dabbling bohemians who wrote and lived with a sense of freedom and rebellion. Among them were Jack Kerouac, Allen Ginsberg, Neal Cassady, Kenneth Rexroth, and Lawrence Ferlinghetti. Ferlinghetti, a prolific publisher of his own poetry and that of his fellow beatniks, opened City Lights Bookstore in San Francisco's North Beach in 1953, establishing a physical hub for a generation of expansive, experimental minds.[127]

WHAT?

The Vesuvio Café is a bohemian mecca built out of a 1913 Italian Renaissance Revival building. The bar, still open at the time of this writing, has maintained its status as an institution for literary minds, thirsty bohemians, freelancers, tourists, and everyone who belongs to the cult of Kerouac. (Vesuvio, in fact, came close to being renamed Kerouac's.) The café itself is a work of art; murals from a beloved local artist adorn the facade of the building; stained glass sparkles above the bar. It's little wonder that it captured the hearts of so many poets, storytellers, and searching souls.[128]

WHERE?

Next door to Lawrence Ferlinghetti's City Lights Bookstore, Vesuvio Café sits on a bohemian stretch of San Francisco's North Beach. Situated next to a pedestrian-only alley (renamed Jack Kerouac Alley), Vesuvio is surrounded by murals and street art that incorporates quotes from poetry and literature.[129]

WHEN?

The 1950s marked the heyday of the beatniks, but Vesuvio's cultural significance still holds strong in the twenty-first century; the café is still a welcoming gathering place for lively locals and visitors alike.[130]

WHAT WERE THEY DRINKING?

Kerouac loved margaritas and "wine-spodiodi," a lethal shot of whiskey and port. But the best drink to order at Vesuvio Café is a bohemian coffee—the caffeine will encourage sprawling verse; the brandy will soothe your wandering spirit. Served warm, it's the perfect companion for a foggy San Francisco afternoon.

WINE SPODIODI[131]

---

1 ounce port wine   1 ounce bourbon

Pour ½ ounce of port wine into a shot glass. Top with 1 ounce of bourbon, then layer the remaining ½ ounce of port wine on top of the bourbon.

VESUVIO CAFÉ'S BOHEMIAN COFFEE[132]

2 ounces
Disaronno Originale

1 ounce brandy

Strong coffee

Lemon twist
for garnishing

Combine Disaronno, brandy, and coffee in a heatproof glass.
Garnish with the lemon twist.

Natalie Clifford Barney and Renée Vivien's
CORPSE REVIVER #2

SERVES 1

Among the beverages that she raised to her lips was a cloudy elixir in which floated a cherry harpooned on a toothpick. I laid a hand on her arm and cautioned her.

"Don"t drink it."

"I've tasted it," I said, embarrassed. "It"s . . . deadly. Be careful, it tastes like some kind of vitriol."

I dared not tell her that I suspected a practical joke. She laughed, flashing her white teeth.

Above left: Natalie Clifford Barney

Above right: Renée Vivien

"But these are my own cocktails, ma pethith Coletthe. They are excellent."[133] —Colette on Renée Vivien, *The Pure and the Impure*, 1932

For over sixty years, American-born poet and fragment writer Natalie Clifford Barney welcomed artists, intellectuals, and writers into her Parisian home, establishing one of the great salons of the late nineteenth and early twentieth centuries.[134] Though Barney never established great fame or acclaim as a writer in the United States, as an ex-pat she was a key figure in the intellectual and artistic movements that swept through Paris at the turn of the century and once more after World War I. She counted among her friends Gertrude Stein and Alice B. Toklas, Ezra Pound, Virgil Thompson, James Joyce, T. S. Eliot, Ernest Hemingway, and more.[135] An openly gay woman, Barney held court with several lesbian and bisexual writers, fostering the careers and social lives of Djuna Barnes, Colette, Sylvia Beach, and Renée Vivien, the British imagist poet who would become one of Barney's lovers.[136] Vivien in particular was known to enjoy frighteningly stiff cocktails.[137]

1 ounce gin

1 ounce Lillet Blanc

1 ounce Cointreau

1 ounce lemon juice, freshly squeezed

1 splash absinthe

Maraschino cherry for garnishing

In a cocktail shaker filled with ice, combine gin, Lillet Blanc, Cointreau, lemon juice, and absinthe, and shake to combine. Strain into a coupe glass. Garnish with the cherry.

Right: Natalie Clifford Barney

Noël Coward's
HORSE'S NECK

SERVES 1

Noël Coward's variation on the Horse's Neck, a classic Prohibition-era cocktail, appears in the lines of his 1951 play *Relative Values* and is touted as the ultimate hangover fix.[138] Bitters and ginger ale will settle your stomach, the aspirin will clear your head, and the brandy will soothe your soul.

1 ½ ounces brandy
3 dashes angostura bitters
Ginger ale
Three aspirin

In a collins glass, combine brandy and angostura bitters and stir. Add ice and top with ginger ale. Serve with three aspirin on the side.

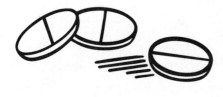

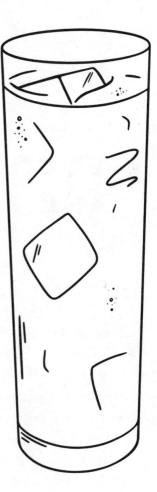

1904 ┄ ┄ ┄ 1973

Pablo Neruda's
EL COQUETELON
AND PISCO SOUR

SERVES 1

Visitors to Pablo Neruda's art deco home in Valparaiso, Chile, enjoyed his house cocktail, El Coquetelon.[139] The poet and diplomat collected colored glass bottles, shells, animal figurines, and friends. If he counted you among them, you might know well the sight of Neruda in a red waiter's jacket pouring you a glass of his effervescent invention.[140]

EL COQUETELON

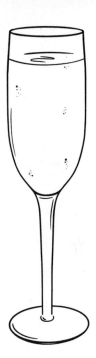

1 ounce cognac

½ ounce Cointreau

2 ounces orange juice,
freshly squeezed

Combine cognac, Cointreau, and orange
juice in a cocktail shaker with ice. Shake
to combine. Pour into a flute glass or a
coupe glass and top with champagne.

PISCO SOUR

The Nobel Prize–winning poet also adored pisco, the national
drink of both Peru and Chile, his home. To Neruda, pisco was
"un millón de años de sol, en una sola gota," or, "a million years of
sun, in a single drop."[141]

3 ounces pisco (preferably a Chilean variety like Alto del Carmen)	1 ounce lime juice, freshly squeezed ¾ ounce simple syrup (1 part sugar dissolved in 1 part water)	1 egg white 1 dash angostura bitters

In a cocktail shaker without ice, combine pisco, lime juice, simple syrup, and egg white. Shake until mixture is foamy. Add ice and shake again until chilled. Strain into a chilled glass—a rocks glass or coupe glass is fine; some prefer a flute. Top with a dash of angostura bitters.

PAIR WITH: *el completo chileno*: a hot dog loaded with mashed avocado, tomato, hot sauce, onions, mayonnaise, mustard, and ketchup and served on a soft bun.[142]

1918 – – 1974

Jacqueline Susann's
2 RED DOLLS AND A SHOT OF SCOTCH

SERVES 1

Jacqueline Susann's novel *Valley of the Dolls* was passed over by several publishers and left to languish at the bottom of the slush pile before it was eventually published in 1966.[143] Luckily, Susann had perfected a cocktail to carry her through the rounds of insecurity and rejection that pummel writers. To soothe a shattered career, she would turn to "two red dolls and a shot of Scotch."[144] The "dolls" that Susann referred to were probably some sort of narcotic, well-versed as she was in the realm of pharmaceuticals and addiction.[145] Our spin on her famous remedy will quell the nagging voice of self-doubt, stoking instead the fires of ambition.

| 2 Atomic FireBall hard candies | 2 ounces Scotch whisky |

Place hard candies at the bottom of a rocks glass. Top with Scotch. Let sit for a couple minutes. Live in the pain and desolation of your rejection. They don't understand you. They aren't ready for what you offer. One day the world will be sorry. Drink the whisky. That burn? It will cleanse you. You're up there—with Warhol, with Capote, with the Beatles. You are the voice of your generation. You'll show them.

Sylvia Plath
and Anne Sexton's
VODKA MARTINI

SERVES 1

The one we talked of so often each time
We downed three extra-dry martinis in Boston.[146]
—Ann Sexton, "Sylvia's Death," 1964

After grueling poetry workshops, Plath and Sexton would head to the Ritz-Carlton in Boston and order—at least— three vodka martinis each, grappling with criticism, their instructor Robert Lowell, and the jagged edges of their psyches that longed for death.[147] Perhaps you too, reader, have craved

Above left: Sylvia Plath
Above right: Anne Sexton

an ice-cold, astringent fix at the end of a brutal, soul-baring day. A drink as bracing as their verse, and as spare—the vodka martini. Just like in poetry, we are down to the bones here. The quality of each component matters dearly.

3 ounces vodka

1 teaspoon
dry vermouth (Dolin)

Lemon twist
for garnishing (optional)

Olive for garnishing (optional)

In a large mixing glass filled with ice, combine vodka and vermouth and stir. Strain into a chilled coupe glass. Garnish with the twist, olive, or both. Repeat. Repeat.

1881 – – 1975

P. G. Wodehouse's
MAY QUEEN AND
GREEN SWIZZLE

SERVES 1

Do we by any chance know of a beverage called May Queen? Its
full name is "Tomorrow'll be all the year the maddest, merriest day
for I'm to be Queen of the May, mother, I'm to be the Queen of the
May."[148] —*Uncle Fred in the Springtime*, 1939

True to its long-form title, Wodehouse's imaginative
concoction, found in the pages of his novel *Uncle Fred in
the Springtime*, is both maddening and merrymaking—filled
with expensive liqueurs and topped with a double hit of
effervescence from stout and champagne.

MAY QUEEN

½ ounce brandy

½ ounce Armagnac

½ ounce kümmel

½ ounce
yellow chartreuse

2 ounces old stout

2 ounces
dry champagne

Combine brandy, Armagnac, kümmel, and chartreuse in a pint glass. Top with stout and champagne.

NOTE: Kümmel is a sweet, colorless liqueur flavored with caraway seeds, cumin, and fennel that dates to sixteenth-century Holland. It is popular in the UK at golf clubs, where its nerve-fighting ability has earned it the nickname of "putting mixture."[149]

Green Swizzle

I have never been in the West Indies, but I am in a position to state that in certain of the fundamentals of life they are streets ahead of our European civilization. That man behind the counter, as kindly a bloke as I ever wish to meet, seemed to guess our requirements the moment we hove in view. Scarcely had our elbows touched the wood before he was leaping to and fro, bringing down a new bottle with each leap. A planter, apparently, does not consider he has had a drink unless it contains at least seven ingredients, and I'm not saying, mind you, that he isn't right. The man behind the bar told us the things were called Green Swizzles; and, if I ever marry and have a song, Green Swizzle Wooster is the name that will go down on the register, in memory of the day his father's life was saved at Wembley.[150] —"The Rummy Affair of Old Biffy," 1924

1 ½ ounces light rum	¼ ounce absinthe	3 dashes angostura bitters
½ ounce overproof rum	1 teaspoon green crème de menthe	Mint sprig for garnishing
1 ounce Velvet falernum	½ ounce lime juice, freshly squeezed	Lime wedge for garnishing

Combine the rums, falernum, absinthe, crème de menthe, and lime juice in a cocktail shaker with cracked ice. Shake, then strain into a collins glass filled two-thirds of the way with crushed ice. Swizzle with a swizzle stick or stir with a barspoon by spinning it between your palms, moving it up and down, until the glass becomes frosty. Add more ice to fill the glass and top the cocktail with angostura bitters. Garnish with the mint sprig and lime wedge. Serve with a metal straw.

Agatha Christie's
PINK GIN

SERVES 1

I t's no mystery that Agatha Christie's best-selling novels pair well with gin. While Christie herself led an abstemious life (perhaps the lack of alcoholic indulgence explains her prolific writing career),[151] Christie's iconic protagonists Hercule Poirot and Miss Marple both enjoyed the occasional tipple before, after, and during their detective work.[152] Pink gin, made with Plymouth gin and a simple dash of angostura bitters, is as classically British as Christie herself.[153]

| 3 dashes
angostura bitters | 2 ounces gin
(preferably Plymouth) |

Add angostura bitters to a chilled rocks glass and swirl to coat. Pour off excess. Add gin and crushed ice.

1911 — 1979

Elizabeth Bishop's
CAIPIRINHA

SERVES 1

We drank cachaça and smoked
the green cheroots. The room
filled with gray-green smoke
and my head couldn't have been dizzier.[154]
—"The Riverman," 1960

B ishop would have enjoyed Brazil's national drink when
she lived in Rio de Janeiro. Made from cachaça—which,
like rum, is a liquor derived from sugarcane, and unlike rum,
can be produced only from freshly pressed sugarcane juice as
opposed to molasses—the caipirinha retains a tell-tale grassy

funkiness.[155] Cachaça must be aged in barrels made from Brazilian wood;[156] like Bishop's poetry from her time in South America, it celebrates a definitive spirit of place.[157]

Bishop's favorite cachaça was called Tatu, its bottle emblazoned with the image of an armadillo—the same animal that would be the subject and title of her famous poem for Robert Lowell.[158]

| 1 lime | 2 ounces cachaça |
| 2 teaspoons sugar | Lime wedge for garnishing |

Cut lime into quarters. In a rocks glass, combine lime quarters and sugar and muddle. Add ice to glass and pour in the cachaça. Stir to combine, and garnish with the lime wedge.

1890 —— 1980

Katherine Anne Porter's
SLOE GIN RICKEY

SERVES 1

Well—as to drinking. I don't know why beer and wine taste so good and are so heavenly to have, but I do know they are. But five bottles of beer in one sitting is a lot of beer for anybody, three are all I ever attempted at my boldest, and your four seem to have done wonders for you. Drink for fun, darling, for sometimes it is fun, and try not to drink just to knock yourself out, because as you have said, it builds up a headache and sometimes makes trouble and in general is no good, no good at all.[159] —Katherine Anne Porter in a letter to her nephew, Paul Porter, 1942

Katherine Anne Porter was a Texas-born journalist, essayist, short story writer, and celebrant of booze, coffee, and cigarettes. Her letters reveal an essential appreciation for the sensual world and all of the primal pleasures within it—its bourbon, its beer, its bloody steaks. Known to enjoy sherry from a snifter, whiskey before dinner, and beer with friends, Porter was also taken with the concept of locally sourcing her ingredients. During a five-month stay in Bermuda, she was delighted to find a nearby lime tree, perfect for brightening her go-to sloe gin rickeys.[160]

2 ounces sloe gin (see recipe page 188)

1 ounce lime juice, freshly squeezed

4 ounces soda water

Lime wedge for garnishing

In a collins glass combine sloe gin and lime juice. Add ice and top with soda water. Garnish with the lime wedge.

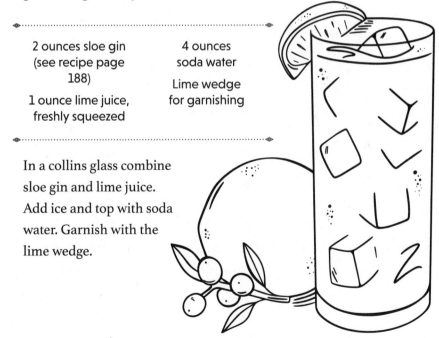

THE HARLEM RENAISSANCE: POETRY, PERFORMANCE, AND HARLEM NIGHT CLUBS

Jazz boys, jazz boys—
Play, plAY , PLAY!
Tomorrow. . . . Is darkness.
Joy today![161]
—Langston Hughes, "Harlem Night Club," 1926

As the 1920s swung into gear, the great migration of blacks from the American south injected northern cities with new life, ideas, and energy. Manhattan's Harlem neighborhood was ground zero for a sweeping cultural and artistic renaissance led by African American luminaries like Zora Neale Hurston, Countee Cullen, Gwendolyn B. Bennett,

Langston Hughes, and a coterie of playwrights, poets, novelists, sculptors, painters, and musicians.

At the time of its renaissance, Harlem was known for its nightclubs, cabarets, and speakeasies—most of which embraced the neighborhood's predominantly African American population. Despite Prohibition, cocktail culture flourished. The neighborhood even developed its own specialty: the Harlem Cocktail, a refreshing gin- and pineapple-based concoction that is equal parts sweet and sour.[162] It was served at the Cotton Club, a bustling nightclub where performers like Duke Ellington, Lena Horne, and Dorothy Dandridge played sold-out shows for all-white audiences. The Cotton Club was not only segregated; it was designed to resemble a plantation. Black performers were told to play "jungle" music and to condescend themselves to the white patrons. After the shows, musicians and waitstaff—who were barred from patronizing the very club they worked at due to Jim Crow laws—would go next door to the basement of 646 Lenox, where they shared corn whiskey and peach brandy.[163]

> White people began to come to Harlem in droves. For several years they packed the expensive Cotton Club on Lenox Avenue. But I was never there, because the Cotton Club was a Jim Crow

club for gangsters and monied whites. They were not cordial to Negro patronage, unless you were a celebrity like Bojangles. So Harlem Negroes did not like the Cotton Club and never appreciated its Jim Crow policy in the very heart of their dark community. Nor did ordinary Negroes like the growing influx of whites toward Harlem after sundown, flooding the little cabarets and bars where formerly only colored people laughed and sang, and where now the strangers were given the best ringside tables to sit and stare at the Negro customers—like amusing animals in a zoo.[164]

—Langston Hughes, *The Big Sea*, 1940

Right: Langston Hughes

Langston Hughes's and Gwendolyn B. Bennett's
HARLEM COCKTAIL

SERVES 1

Langston Hughes regularly drank beer and whiskey, but he surely enjoyed his fair share of his beloved neighborhood's eponymous cocktail.[165] Perhaps he would have tossed a few back in the company of his good friend Gwendolyn B. Bennett, a poet and painter who, along with Hughes, was the cofounder of the short-lived but culturally significant literary journal *Fire!!* and founded Harlem Circles, spaces for young Harlem writers including Countee Cullen, Eric Walrond, Helene Johnson, and Zora Neale Hurston to comingle, commiserate, and create— perhaps over cocktails.[166]

Above left: Langston Hughes
Above right: Gwendolyn B. Bennett

1 ½ ounces dry gin	3 dashes	Pineapple chunk
¾ ounce	maraschino liqueur	for garnishing
pineapple juice		

In a cocktail shaker, combine gin, pineapple juice, and maraschino liqueur. Add ice. Shake vigorously until well chilled. Strain into a chilled coupe glass. Skewer the pineapple with a toothpick and place in drink to garnish.

Tennessee Williams's
RAMOS GIN FIZZ

 SERVES 1

T ennessee Williams led a troubled life, ameliorated at
times and made worse at others by his lifelong allegiance
to brandy and barbiturates.[167] Williams's affection for these
substances would see his demise; in many ways, the tragic
romanticism that informs his plays *A Streetcar Named Desire* and
The Glass Menagerie played out in his own life.[168] He struggled
to contend with his sexuality, battled with a dependence
on substances, and alienated himself through histrionics.[169]
Depressed yet? Time for a "drinky-pie," as Williams was known
to call them.

2 ounces gin	½ ounce lemon juice, freshly squeezed	2 teaspoons superfine sugar
1 ounce heavy cream		2 or 3 drops orange blossom water
1 egg white	½ ounce lime juice, freshly squeezed	Splash club soda

In a cocktail shaker, combine all ingredients except club soda with ice and shake vigorously. Strain into a collins glass and top with a splash of club soda. Enjoy on a balmy New Orleans night. Limit yourself to two, lest you feel the urge to start shouting "Stella!" from your balcony.

1924 — 1984

Truman Capote's
ORANGE DRINKS

SERVES 1

The test of whether or not a writer has divined the natural shape of his story is just this: after reading it, can you imagine it differently, or does it silence your imagination and seem to you absolute and final? As an orange is final. As an orange is something nature has made just right.[170] —Interview with the *Paris Review*, No. 16 (Spring–Summer 1957)

Over the course of his migration from Monroeville, Alabama, to Manhattan, Truman Capote, born Truman Streckfus Persons, developed discerning tastes.[171] Both of these drinks can be served for breakfast—and not just at Tiffany's. But if you elect to start your day with My Orange Drink instead of the Capotiana, we implore you to [Holly] go lightly.

Capotiana (for sober days)

| 1 part orange juice, freshly squeezed | 1 part tomato juice |

Combine equal parts orange and tomato juices in a tumbler. No ice.

My Orange Drink (for the rest)

2 ounces vodka

4 ounces orange juice, freshly squeezed

Maraschino cherry for garnishing

Orange slice for garnishing

Combine vodka and orange juice in a tumbler filled with ice and stir. Garnish with the cherry and orange slice.

1899 — 1985

E. B. White's
MARTINI AND POMPIER*

SERVES 1

Children's author, essayist, and Pulitzer Prize winner E. B. White is still the authority on *The Elements of Style*. Though his take on a martini lacks the austerity and dry bite of the classic version, his idiosyncratic recipe is still smooth, unfussy, and perfectly clear—just like the prose he championed.[172]

1 ½ teaspoons apricot brandy	1 ½ teaspoons lime juice, freshly squeezed	1 ½ teaspoons honey
1 ½ teaspoons dry vermouth		2 ounces gin

---

* Adapted from the letters of E. B. White

In a cocktail mixing glass, stir together apricot brandy, vermouth, lime juice, and honey. Add ice and gin, stir, and strain into a chilled coupe glass.

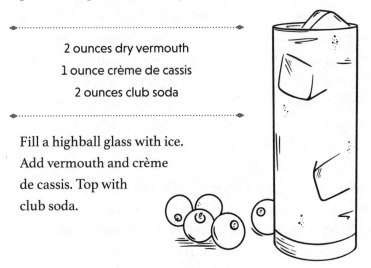

POMPIER

On the rare occasion that a martini, or as White dubbed it, "the elixir of quietude,"[173] inhibits productivity, choose instead the Pompier: a refreshing, low-alcohol highball that will clear the proverbial cobwebs and put a little spritz in your step.[174]

2 ounces dry vermouth
1 ounce crème de cassis
2 ounces club soda

Fill a highball glass with ice. Add vermouth and crème de cassis. Top with club soda.

1908 ——————— 1986

Simone de Beauvoir's
APRICOT COCKTAILS

SERVES 1

It remains a mystery what comprised the apricot cocktails that so entranced Simone de Beauvoir at the Bec-de-Gaz on the Rue Montparnasse.[175] They were the house specialty, and the source of philosophical musings for de Beauvoir and her crew of fellow existentialists, like Jean-Paul Sartre (her longtime partner), Raymond Aron, and Albert Camus.[176] The cocktail served as a key to understanding phenomenology: it existed to be enjoyed and it existed *because* it was enjoyed.[177] These two versions of the apricot cocktail hinge on de Beauvoir's favorite spirits: vodka and whiskey.[178] Both are booze-forward, slightly sweet, and emanate an amber glow. Take your pick. Existentialism, after all, hinges on the freedom of choice.

THE SECOND SEX

1 ½ ounces vodka

½ ounce dry vermouth

2 ½ teaspoons apricot liqueur

1 dash angostura bitters

In a cocktail mixer or large mixing glass filled with ice, combine vodka, vermouth, apricot liqueur, and bitters. Stir well, until you get a whiff of apricot. Strain into a chilled coupe glass.

The Woman Destroyed

1 ½ ounces Scotch whisky

¾ ounce sweet vermouth

½ ounce apricot liqueur

¼ ounce Cynar

Lemon peel
for garnishing

In a cocktail mixer or large mixing glass filled with ice, combine whiskey, vermouth, apricot liqueur, and Cynar, and stir well to combine. Strain into a chilled coupe glass. Garnish with the lemon peel.

NOTE: Cynar is an Italian bitter of the amaro variety derived from herbs and plants, predominantly artichoke.

THE WHITE HORSE TAVERN

WHO?

James Baldwin, Dylan Thomas, Anaïs Nin, William Styron, Norman Mailer, Allen Ginsberg, John Ashbery, and Jack Kerouac were just some of the great literary minds who frequented the Greenwich Village pub during its heyday in the middle of the twentieth century. James Baldwin was a regular, enjoying whiskies from his usual seat at the bar. Jack Kerouac was another matter. He was so frequently unruly that someone took the liberty of carving the words "JACK GO HOME!" on a bathroom stall.[179]

WHAT?

"The Horse," as its patrons lovingly called it, was a popular hangout for New York's bohemian crowd. Established in 1880, the bar was initially known as a place for longshoremen to gather after work, and as the twentieth century took off, became a beloved watering hole for writers.[180]

WHERE?

The White Horse Tavern sits at the corner of Hudson and West 11th Street in New York's Greenwich Village, in the beating heart of what was, at the time of its opening, a working-class, immigrant-rich neighborhood.[181]

WHEN?

The Horse opened in 1880 but it reached its literary heyday in the middle of the twentieth century.[182]

WHAT WERE THEY DRINKING?

The White Horse Tavern was a no-frills dive and the drinks followed suit. Neat whiskies and draft beers were safe bets. Welsh poet Dylan Thomas famously spent an evening at the Horse drinking whiskey after whiskey—eighteen, as legend holds—until he stumbled outside, collapsed on the street, was taken to a hospital uptown, and perished three days later.[183]

1924 — 1987

James Baldwin's
BOURBON, NEAT

SERVES 1

If you decide (and you should) to forego Dylan Thomas's eighteen whiskeys, model your order instead after *Notes of a Native Son* author and White Horse Tavern regular James Baldwin and keep it simple with a bourbon, neat.[184]

---

2 ounces bourbon

Pour 2 ounces of bourbon into a rocks glass. After, gather a group of friends and head to El Faro, a Spanish restaurant Baldwin frequented in the village. Pick up the check; Baldwin was known for his generosity.[185]

1938 — 1988

Raymond Carver's
"HEART STARTER"
BLOODY MARY

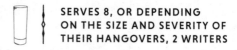

**SERVES 8, OR DEPENDING
ON THE SIZE AND SEVERITY OF
THEIR HANGOVERS, 2 WRITERS**

Perhaps, when the University of Iowa took Raymond Carver and John Cheever on as faculty for the school's prestigious graduate creative writing program, the administration imagined that the fiction writers would tend to the well-being and creative nourishment of their students. But Carver and Cheever made fast, close, and reckless friends, drinking with a fervor that far outpaced their writing. "He and I did nothing but drink," Carver said of the time he spent on faculty with Cheever. "I don't think either of us ever took the covers off our typewriters."[186] To nurse the frequent hangovers that followed their booze-soaked evenings, Carver turned to the Bloody Mary.[187] This one includes one of his favorite bar snacks as a garnish, a cocktail shrimp.[188]

4 cups
tomato juice

½ cup dill
pickle juice

¼ cup lemon juice,
freshly squeezed

1 tablespoon
grated horseradish

2 teaspoons
Tabasco sauce

2 teaspoons
Worcestershire
sauce

1 teaspoon
kosher salt

1 teaspoon
freshly ground
black pepper

½ teaspoon
celery seeds

⅛ teaspoon
cayenne
pepper

2 cups vodka

Celery stalks
for garnishing

Lemon wedges
for garnishing

Cocktail shrimp
for garnishing

In a large pitcher, mix together tomato juice, pickle juice, lemon juice, horseradish, Tabasco, Worcestershire, salt, pepper, celery seeds, and cayenne pepper. Cover and chill in refrigerator overnight.

In the morning (or whenever it is you wake up), locate your phone, keys, dignity, and pants. Next, find the vodka (if you have any left), and pour it into the tomato juice mixture. Stir. Pour into a highball or collins glass filled with ice and garnish with celery, a lemon wedge, and a cocktail shrimp.

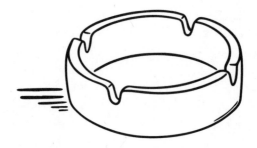

Richard Hughes's
and Anthony Burgess's
HANGMAN'S BLOOD

SERVES 1

A s its name might suggest, this precursor to the Long Island iced tea is not for the faint of heart. First described by Welsh author, poet, and playwright Richard Hughes in his pirate novel *A High Wind in Jamaica*,[189] the Hangman's Blood was also a favorite of *A Clockwork Orange* author Anthony Burgess. "It tastes very smooth, induces a somewhat metaphysical elation, and rarely leaves a hangover," he relayed to the *Guardian* in 1960. "I recommend this for a quick, though expensive, lift."[190]

Above left: Richard Hughes
Above right: Anthony Burgess

Hangman's Blood . . . is compounded of rum, gin, brandy, and porter. . . . Innocent (merely beery) as it looks, refreshing as it tastes, it has the property of increasing rather than allaying thirst and so once it has made a breach, soon demolishes the whole fort.[191]

—Richard Hughes, *A High Wind in Jamaica*, 1929

2 ounces rum	2 ounces brandy	1 small bottle of stout
2 ounces gin	2 ounces port	
2 ounces whiskey		Champagne

Pour the liquors and port into a pint glass. Add a small bottle of stout. Top with champagne.

NOTE: leave no room for ice.

Charles Bukowski's
BOILERMAKER

SERVES 1

When you drank the world was still out there, but for the moment it didn't have you by the throat.[192] —*Factotum*, 1975

It makes sense that Charles Bukowski's stories and poems reside in back alleys, dirty dive bars, and the gritty corners of downtown Los Angeles. Bukowski began drinking heavily at thirteen, and never really let up.[193] He unabashedly embraced the unglamorous lifestyle of vagrants and alcoholics, despite the fame and success that he eventually encountered. At the age of thirty-five, doctors advised him against drinking: his liver was shot, he wouldn't survive his boozy lifestyle.[194] Still, he maintained a fealty to the bottle, writing endlessly about the dingy bars, sexual encounters, and hangovers that punctuated his days until he died nearly forty years later.[195]

| 2 ounces bourbon | 1 pint light beer |

Pour bourbon into a shot glass. Pour a pint of light beer (anything but Coors—Bukowski's least favorite). Drop the shot into the pint glass. Repeat as necessary.

1922 — — 1995

Kingsley Amis's
TUFT OF THE DOG,
OR A POLISH BISON*

SERVES 1

About 12:30, firmly take a hair (or better, in Cyril Connolly's phrase, a tuft) of the dog that bit you. The dog, by the way, is of no particular breed: there is no obligation to go for the same drink as the one you were mainly punishing the night before.[196] —*Everyday Drinking*, 2008

Kingsley Amis, "The Laureate of the Hangover," was known to claim Macallan 10 as his desert island drink of choice.[197] But the next mornings, often doomed by hangovers of the

---

* Adapted from *Everyday Drinking: The Distilled Kingsley Amis*

"metaphysical" and "physical" variety, called for a hearty, warm, and savory tipple.[198]

3 ounces Bovril beef bouillon

¾ to 1 cup hot water

1 ½ ounces vodka

2 dashes Worcestershire sauce

1 dash lemon juice

Dissolve Bovril in hot water in a mug. Add vodka, Worcestershire sauce, and lemon juice. Sip until "that ineffable compound of depression, sadness (those two are not the same), anxiety, self-hatred, sense of failure and fear for the future" fades.

Eudora Welty's
MOTHER'S EGGNOG

SERVES 1

There was a birthday cake with candles, & presents of preserves,
jelly, etc., plus a beautiful gold pin with my initials, the date, &
"Losing Battles" on it—wasn't that grand? I didn't mean to leave out
the bourbon, there was lots of that too.[199] —Eudora Welty in a letter
to Mary Louise Aswell, *Eudora Welty: A Biography*, 2015

It follows that the beloved southern writer, winner of the
Presidential Medal of Freedom and the Pulitzer Prize in
fiction for her novella *The Optimist's Daughter*, preferred a
drink with the same spirit of place that fills her fiction.[200] Her
ideal day ended with a few ounces of bourbon and a splash of
water[201]—or, "wahtah," as she pronounced it in her Mississippi

drawl.[202] And her daily life matched in its simplicity: waking early, drinking coffee (stopping at eleven, lest it keep her up all night), reading, writing, checking into local haunts (a Greek restaurant in Jackson, her favorite), sipping her bourbon, and watching the evening news to unwind.[203] But Eudora Welty, who welcomed others into her home with the quiet, gracious sense of a true entertainer, left a trove of beloved recipes behind.[204] The recipe for her eggnog, served on Christmas morning, has the richness of the holiday treat, with a nod to her roots in the addition of bourbon.[205]

6 egg yolks,
well beaten

3 tablespoons
powdered sugar,
sifted

1 cup bourbon

1 pint heavy
whipping cream

6 egg whites,
whipped

Nutmeg,
freshly grated,
for garnishing

Combine yolks and powdered sugar in a saucepan and warm over low heat. Stir in bourbon slowly, beating all the while. Add whipping cream. Stir to combine, then fold in egg whites. Top with the nutmeg. Pair with a festive and bourbon-laden dessert, like Eudora's family's favorite white fruit cake.

WHITE FRUIT CAKE[206]

4 cups sifted flour, and more flour for dusting

½ pound candied red cherries

½ pound candied green cherries

1 pound candied pineapple

1 pound pecans

1 ½ cups unsalted butter

2 cups sugar

2 teaspoons baking powder

⅛ teaspoon salt

6 large eggs, yolks separated from whites

1 cup bourbon

1 teaspoon vanilla extract

Preheat oven to 250 degrees F. Grease three medium-sized Bundt cake pans and dust with flour. Halve fruits. Chop half of pecans, reserving the rest to use as a topping. Dust fruit and nuts with flour.

In the bowl of a large stand mixer fitted with the paddle attachment, cream butter and sugar on medium speed.

Sift together flour, baking powder, and salt.

Begin adding flour mixture and egg yolks to the butter-sugar mixture, adding ⅔ cup of the flour mixture and 1 egg yolk to the bowl at a time, and repeating until all dry ingredients and egg yolks are mixed in.

With the mixer running, add the chopped pecans to the bowl, then add ⅓ cup bourbon. Add the pineapple and another

⅓ cup bourbon. Next, add the cherries, the remaining ⅓ cup bourbon, and the vanilla.

By hand or using a mixer, whip egg whites until stiff peaks form. Fold into the batter.

Place the reserved pecans on the bottom of the cake pans. Pour batter into cake pans, filling about two-thirds of the way.

Bake for 3 hours, or until the tops of the cakes spring to the touch and a toothpick inserted at the center comes out clean.

According to Eudora, "you may improve [the cake] with a little more bourbon, dribbled over the top to be absorbed and [to] ripen the cake before cutting."[207]

1933 — — 2004

Susan Sontag's
LIST OF LIKES

SERVES 1

Here, the cocktail emerges as a compilation, elevated by its discrete parts. The ingredients borrow from one of Sontag's famous lists of things she likes.[208] Even though she famously wrote *Against Interpretation*, we would hope that she would accept the liberties we've taken with some of her favorite things.

1 serrano pepper, seeded	1 ½ ounces wheatgrass juice	Sugarcane stalk for garnishing
1 small piece of ginger root	¾ ounce lime juice, freshly squeezed	Slice of green apple for garnishing
1 ½ ounces tequila	½ ounce simple syrup	

Thinly slice serrano pepper and roughly chop ginger. Muddle at the bottom of a rocks glass. Add tequila, wheatgrass, lime juice, simple syrup, and ice. Stir with a straw or barspoon. Garnish with the sugarcane and slice of green apple.

Hunter S. Thompson's
SINGAPORE SLING
(with a side of mezcal and a beer chaser)

SERVES 1

Hunter S. Thompson garnered fame for blurring the lines of fiction and reality; within his reporting and storytelling, he merged fact, experience, exaggeration, and satire, couching it under the umbrella of gonzo journalism.[209] Throughout his writing life, Thompson kept odd hours and hard habits. According to his biographer E. Jean Carroll, Hunter had his morning cocaine *before* he took his coffee. (Morning, we should note, often began at 3 p.m.) After some Chivas Regal, a few glasses of orange juice, a handful of Dunhills, more coffee, and yes, more cocaine, the eccentric writer was set to begin his day's work at around midnight. Interrupted only by occasional hits of acid, Dove ice-cream bars, intermittent dips in a hot tub, and a continuous stream of pornographic movies, Thompson toiled diligently until morning—when he'd finally crawl to sleep.[210]

Thompson's seminal autobiographical novel, *Fear and Loathing in Las Vegas: A Savage Journey to the Heart of the American Dream*, perfectly captures his wild-man, gonzo spirit, complete with its jaw-dropping, stranger-than-fiction depictions of wild nights (and mornings, and afternoons) as well as eccentric characters.[211] In the 1971 roman à clef, Raoul Duke, Thompson's booze-swilling, drug-bingeing stand-in, consumes his beverages with calculated vigor. Mix yourself a Singapore sling[212]—and don't forget the mezcal and beer chaser—and you'll be ready to embark on your own savage journey.[213]

1 ½ ounces London dry gin	¾ ounce pineapple juice	Mint spring for garnishing
¼ ounce Cointreau	¼ ounce grenadine (see recipe page 103)	
¼ ounce Cherry Heering		**On the side:**
¼ ounce Benedictine	1 dash angostura bitters	2 ounces mezcal, neat
1 ounce lime juice, freshly squeezed	Soda water	Budweiser, cold
	Fresh fruit for garnishing	

Combine gin, Cointreau, Cherry Heering, Benedictine, lime juice, pineapple juice, grenadine, and angostura bitters in a cocktail shaker. Add ice, shake until well-chilled, and strain into a collins glass filled with ice. Top with soda water. Garnish with the fresh fruit and mint sprig. Serve with a shot of mezcal and a can of Bud.

1923 — 2007

Norman Mailer's
BERLIN STATION
CHIEF

SERVES 1

Journalist, essayist, playwright, and novelist Norman Mailer often drank as a warm-up to writing, stating, "I usually need a can of beer to prime me."[214] The pre-writing drink worked as an auspicious ritual for Mailer; he reached great renown as a journalist and fiction writer, lauded for his rich storytelling and imaginative depth.[215] Perhaps he created the Berlin Station Chief while he contemplated the beginning of his writing day. The smoky martini first appeared in his 1991 novel *Harlot's Ghost*.[216] Unlike a traditional martini, this cocktail utilizes single-malt Scotch in place of vermouth, imparting a sultry, peaty finish.

2 ounces gin

1 ounce single-malt Scotch

Lemon twist
for garnishing

In a mixing glass, combine gin and Scotch and add ice. Stir to combine. Strain into a chilled coupe glass and garnish with the lemon twist.

1932 — 2009

John Updike's
OLD-FASHIONED

SERVES 1

John Updike didn't fall into the same traps of overindulgence that plagued other writers of his era; he practiced moderation throughout his life and was rewarded by a long and successful publishing career.[217] However, the old-fashioned featured crucially in his 1960 novel *Rabbit, Run*, proving Updike's familiarity with cocktails of the time.[218] But while the cocktail played a key role in the novel's domestic tragedy, it would transcend these fraught associations, becoming part and parcel of the craft cocktail renaissance of the twenty-first century.[219]

| 1 sugar cube | 2 ounces bourbon |
| 2 dashes angostura bitters | Orange peel for garnishing |

In a double rocks glass, muddle sugar cube with angostura bitters. Add bourbon and 1 large ice cube and stir with a barspoon to combine. Garnish with the orange peel.

1919 — — 2010

J. D. Salinger's
SCOTCH AND SODA

 SERVES 1

> I ordered a Scotch and soda and told him not to mix it—I said it
> fast as hell, because if you hem and haw, they think you're under
> twenty-one and won't sell you any intoxicating liquor.[220]
> —*The Catcher in the Rye*, 1951

J. D. Salinger was famously reclusive. After he reached critical
and commercial success with 1951's *Catcher in the Rye*, he
retreated to New Hampshire, where he lived out his life in
privacy, shrouding his alleged eccentricities and obsessions
from the world—some innocuous (eating frozen peas for breakfast) and some disturbing (allegedly drinking his own urine for

health benefits).[221] What's certain amidst all of the rumors that surround the mysterious writer's life is that he carried many of the same anxieties and antisocial tendencies of Holden Caulfield, *The Catcher in the Rye*'s teenaged protagonist.[222] It's safe to say that Salinger, a self-professed "perennial sad sack," (not unlike Caulfield), would have also ordered Scotch and sodas from the dives around his rural New Hampshire town, given that despite his desire to live in isolation, he did socialize often, carousing around soda bars in the company of local teenagers, particularly the girls. His pickup line? "I'm J. D. Salinger and I wrote *Catcher in the Rye*."[223]

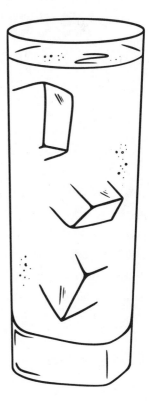

2 ounces Scotch whisky

4 ounces soda water

Pour Scotch into a highball glass. Fill glass with ice. Top with soda water.

1949 – – 2011

Christopher Hitchens's
SCOTCH AND PERRIER

 SERVES 1

According to *Vanity Fair*'s Graydon Carter, Christopher Hitchens "was a man of insatiable appetites—for cigarettes, for Scotch, for company," and "for great writing."[224] Hitchens claimed that his productivity was fortified by his heavy consumption. He produced at least one thousand words a day and never missed a deadline.[225]

| A decent slug of Johnnie Walker | Perrier water |

Combine in a tumbler and drink before noon.

1941 — 2012

Nora Ephron's
KIR

SERVES 1

B orrowing its name from Felix Kir—a World War II resistance fighter and former mayor of Dijon who allegedly mixed black currant liquor with dry white wine after the Nazis confiscated the best Burgundy reds—the kir is a refreshing and acidic predinner drink.[226] Novelist, screenwriter, essayist, and director Nora Ephron preferred this classic French aperitif served with a side of ice.[227]

¼ ounce crème de cassis	Dry, acidic white wine, chilled

Pour crème de cassis into a wine glass and top with white wine.

1922 — — 2012

Helen Gurley Brown's
SKINNY HOT BUTTERED RUM AND CHLOROFORM

SERVES 6

Editor of *Cosmopolitan* and author of *Sex and the Single Girl* Helen Gurley Brown's fixation on the act of consumption was only bested by her fastidious obsession with maintaining a thin appearance; throughout her ninety years, she was known to maintain an obsessive cycle of bingeing and dieting, delighting all weekend in cinnamon buns and ice cream and punishing herself with small spoonfuls of tuna salad and sugar-free Jell-O come Monday.[228] Her cocktails of choice reveal her strident obsession with diet as well as her repressed longing for indulgence, her allegiance to tradition as well as her desire to update it, and her appeal to popular tastes nuanced by an undeniable idiosyncratic streak.[229]

SKINNY HOT BUTTERED RUM

1 tablespoon margarine

1 packet Equal sweetener

1 ounce dark rum

Cloves for garnishing

Combine margarine, Equal, and rum in a mug. Fill with boiling water. Top with a few cloves.

CHLOROFORM[230]

6 cups strong
brewed coffee

12 ½ ounces gin
or vodka

2 pints vanilla
ice cream, melted

10 dashes
orange bitters

Nutmeg,
freshly grated,
for garnishing

Bring the coffee to a boil in a saucepan and boil until it has reduced to a single cup. Let cool to room temperature. Transfer to a large punch bowl and add gin, ice cream, and bitters. Stir to combine and garnish with the nutmeg.

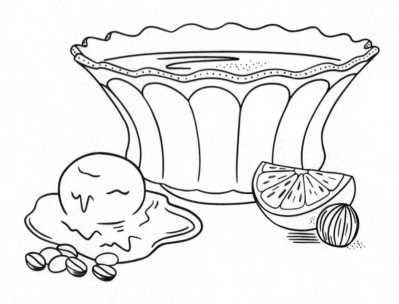

Seamus Heaney's
SLOE GIN

 SERVES 1

This liqueur achieves its gorgeous ruby tint from the infusion of sloe berries, which are usually foraged from blackthorn bushes after the first frost of winter.[231] You will need a large glass jar in which to store the mixture while the berries steep and imbue the gin with their aromatic essence. Some of the instruction here is taken from Heaney's own verse.

> The clear weather of juniper
> darkened into winter.
> She fed gin to sloes
> and sealed the glass container.[232]
> —"Sloe Gin," *Station Island*, 1984

| 2 cups sloe berries | 1 cup sugar | 4 cups (1 liter) gin |

Rinse berries, pat dry, prick with a stainless steel fork or toothpick, and place in a glass jar. Add sugar and gin to the jar, seal, and shake well to combine. Store the sloe gin in a cool, dark place for three months. After three months, strain contents of jar into sanitized, dry bottles using a muslin cloth. Enjoy right away or store for up to one year; the flavor will improve with time.[233]

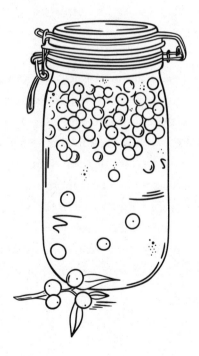

1928 — 2014

Maya Angelou's
SHERRY

SERVES 1

In a 1990 interview with the *Paris Review*, Maya Angelou discussed her ritual of writing in a hotel room accompanied only by the Bible, a thesaurus, a yellow legal pad, an ashtray, and a bottle of sherry.[234] She'd usually have a glass at 11 a.m., but by her own accounting sometimes began imbibing as soon as she arrived at 6:15 in the morning.[235] Angelou's morning tipple never seemed to get in the way of her productivity; she published prolifically, served on two presidential committees, was awarded the Presidential Medal of Freedom by Barack Obama, and earned over fifty honorary degrees before her death.[236] Her recipe for success may have been unconventional and filled with sherry, but it certainly served Angelou—and her nation—well.

1 bottle sherry
The Bible
Roget's Thesaurus
Yellow legal pad
An ashtray

Spread out on top of the hotel bed. Open the bible; read aloud. Pour yourself a glass of sherry.

Jackie Collins's
JACKIE COLLINS COCKTAIL*

SERVES 1

Jackie Collins was a formidable writer: she wrote thirty-two novels, all of which made the *New York Times* best sellers list, and in total sold more than four hundred million copies.[237] Glamorous and gorgeous, Collins delighted readers with lavish worlds doused in crime, sex, and diamonds.[238] This cocktail, effervescent and tart, is nearly as crowd-pleasing as Collins's books.

---

* Adapted from Wolfgang Puck's recipe in Collins's *The Lucky Santangelo Cookbook*, 2014.

6 raspberries	2 ounces vodka	Fresh mint leaf for garnishing
½ ounce simple syrup (1 part sugar dissolved in 1 part water)	2 ounces lemonade	Raspberry for garnishing
	½ lime	
	1 ½ ounces club soda	

In a cocktail shaker, muddle raspberries with the simple syrup. Add vodka and lemonade, then squeeze the lime into the shaker. Add ice and shake vigorously until chilled. Pour in club soda, shake once, and strain into a highball glass over ice. Garnish with the mint leaf and raspberry.

1956 ———————— 2018

Anthony Bourdain's
NEGRONI

 SERVES 1

The late, great chef, food writer, and memoirist Anthony Bourdain was a fan of this classic Italian *aperitivo*.[239] He was drawn to the negroni right away, intrigued by its interplay of bitter, sweet, and botanical notes.[240] Bourdain liked them so much that he whipped up a big pitcher for his television crew one night, complete with an entire bottle each of gin, vermouth, and Campari.[241] Things soon went off the rails—Bourdain vaguely remembered finding a cameraman with his head stuck in the freezer.[242] The boozy negroni, after all, is no session cocktail; it packs a heavy punch. In the words of Bourdain, "those things hit you like a freight train after four or five."[243]

| 1 ounce gin | (preferably Martini & Rossi) | Orange twist for garnishing |
| 1 ounce sweet vermouth | 1 ounce Campari | |

Combine gin, sweet vermouth, and Campari in a mixing glass. Add ice and stir until chilled. Strain over ice (we like one big rock here) into a rocks glass. Garnish with the orange twist.

Eve Babitz's
WHITE LADY

 SERVES 1

> There seemed no place to go, after fourteen White Ladies, but into a spin that fell out of the sky, a smashed victim of impending gravity.[244] —*Sex and Rage*, 1979

E ve Babitz is to the 1960s and 1970s of Los Angeles what Edith Wharton was to New York's Gilded Age. Babitz's thinly veiled novels and autofiction stories captured the unreality of Hollywood and its famous tenants with an attention to sensual detail, candor, and good humor. It's impossible to read Babitz without gaining a sense of her tastes. One need only read the eight-page dedication to her first book, *Eve's Hollywood*.[245] Her drug of choice was anything available; she loved strawberries and asparagus and the way that whipped cream came in a silver gravy dish at the Polo Lounge.[246] She loved tempura and tea cakes and she loved champagne.[247] But where cocktails are concerned, her favorite was the White Lady, a luscious concoction of London dry gin, Cointreau, lemon, and foamy egg whites.[248]

1 ½ ounces gin (London dry)

¾ ounce Cointreau

¾ ounce lemon juice, freshly squeezed

1 egg white

Lemon peel for garnishing

Combine gin, Cointreau, lemon juice, and egg white in a cocktail shaker and shake vigorously. Add ice to shaker and shake until chilled. Strain into a chilled coupe glass and garnish with the lemon peel.

GLORY, THE GRAPE: NORA EPHRON, JOAN DIDION, ALICE MUNRO, MARGUERITE DURAS, LORD BYRON, AND JAY MCINERNEY ON WINE

Let us have wine and woman, mirth and laughter. —Lord Byron

What unites Jay McInerney, Nora Ephron, Joan Didion, Alice Munro, Marguerite Duras, and Lord Byron? A great love of wine.

Modes of appreciation differ; as do preferences. Where Marguerite Duras, author of *The Lover*, was known to pack in as many as eight liters of Bordeaux a day,[249] Nobel Prize–winning short story writer Alice Munro reportedly savors a chilled glass of sauvignon blanc with dinner.[250] Los Angeles's Joan Didion models restraint like Munro, sipping on a glass of wine in the evening while making edits to her day's work.[251] The nineteenth-century poet Lord Byron, who never met a taboo that wasn't worth breaking, drank his wine from a human skull.[252] Upon discovering the unusual receptacle, Nathaniel Hawthorne, author of *The Scarlet Letter* and *The House of the Seven Gables*, remarked, "a man must be either very drunk or very thirsty before he would taste wine out of such a goblet."[253] Byron's verse responds in his typical gleeful, devious logic:

> *And, when alas! our brains are gone,*
> *What nobler substitute than wine?*[254]

For many writers, overindulgence in wine left them withered on the vine. But some have flourished through their appreciation, cultivating writing lives that marry language and craft with taste and discernment. British novelist Julian Barnes and *Bright Lights, Big City* author Jay McInerney discovered a mutual love of wine, embarking on a correspondence that revealed their burgeoning connoisseurship, delighting in ecstatic strophes about Tuscan Sangioveses, Ridge cabernets, and Châteauneuf-du-Papes.[255] Jay McInerney soon found a second career in the wine world, writing about grapes and vintages with a clarity, enjoyment, and relatability that was difficult to find in the existing wine canon.[256]

Tips for Writing about Wine from Jay McInerney

"As with writing about sex," McInerney states, "writing about wine can be hazardous."[257] Altogether, the same pratfalls accompany wine writing and novel writing, and the same methods carry water. "One of the best ways to describe the aesthetic experience of wine is with metaphors and similes," McInerney says, and as with sex writing, leaning too heavily on technical language and breathless descriptions of flora might result in clichéd, pretentious prose.[258]

The eternal workshop mantra holds true: it's best to write what you know.

Descriptions of fruit flavors and floral aromas undoubtedly have their place, but when I found myself in an early column needing to distinguish a Chablis from a Napa chardonnay, I groped with flavor descriptors like citrus and mineral on the one hand, and butter and pineapple on the other. But ultimately comparing the one to Kate Moss and the other to Pamela Anderson seemed to get the job done.[259] —*Town & Country*

Salman Rushdie's
VODKA TONIC

SERVES 1

Salman Rushdie, author of over twenty-five books, including Booker Prize winner *Midnight's Children*, explained to PUNCH magazine that he's become "a rather boring drinker" in his seventies, electing the refreshing and simple vodka tonic as his nightcap of choice.[260] While Rushdie is no stranger to controversy—the Ayatollah Khomeini issued a fatwa against the author in 1989 after the publication of *The Satanic Verses*—his beverage order is a guaranteed safe bet.[261]

2 ounces vodka

3 ounces tonic water

Lime slice
for garnishing

Combine vodka and tonic water in a highball glass over ice. Garnish with the lime slice before serving.

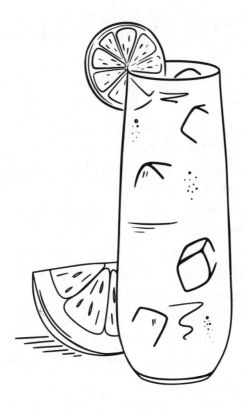

1949

Haruki Murakami's
WHISKY, NEAT

SERVES 1

In the words of celebrated Japanese novelist Haruki Murakami, "Whiskey, like a beautiful woman, demands appreciation. You gaze first, then it's time to drink."[262] Murakami's surrealist fiction reveals his long-held affection for the spirit. The Scottish Cutty Sark finds mention in *The Wind-Up Bird Chronicle* and *1Q84*, and a man named Johnnie Walker (after the Scotch) appears in *Kafka on the Shore*.[263]

Japan has a strong whiskey manufacturing tradition, the island nation being home to Yamazaki, Nikka, and Suntory—each with their loyal fans and high-end vintages. But Murakami also appreciates the Western brands—some of them inexpensive and scoffed at by connoisseurs—that carried him through university and during his time as a barman at jazz clubs.[264]

---

2 ounces Cutty Sark

Pour Cutty Sark into a rocks glass. Savor the whisky while Charlie Parker's sweet saxophone sounds linger on your record player.

Candace Bushnell's
COSMOPOLITAN*

SERVES 1

The New York of Candace Bushnell's *Sex and the City* is redolent in caustic, raunchy wit, smoking sections, and of course, cosmopolitans. Like her protagonist Carrie Bradshaw, Bushnell is known to order the blush pink drink, a classic from the eighties that pairs well with sex talk, best friends, and Manolo Blahniks.[265]

At the tail end of the twentieth century it seemed like there were more cosmopolitans being served up in a single night than single men in New York City. Ordering a cosmo would elicit groans from "serious" bartenders who thought that the drink was overly sweet, overly girlish.[266] But, as Bushnell wrote, "it started

---

* Adapted from Toby Cecchini's original recipe

the way it always does: innocently enough."[267] During his shift at The Odeon in Tribeca, bartender Toby Cecchini whipped up the simple drink for a waitress who'd heard of a similar drink being made in San Francisco.[268] The pink concoction became the staff drink and soon took off throughout the city; it's only natural that it found its way into Bushnell's *New York Observer* column, and then into the carefree grasp of Carrie Bradshaw. In the words of Bushnell herself, "Man may have discovered fire, but women discovered how to play with it."[269]

We like this cocktail as dry as Bushnell's wit, so we've swapped out the traditional Ocean Spray for a tart, unsweetened cranberry juice. Unlike a bad date, this late-century classic will always go down easy.

1 ½ ounces citron vodka
¾ ounce Cointreau
¾ ounce lime juice, freshly squeezed
¾ ounce unsweetened cranberry juice
Lemon peel for garnishing

Fill a cocktail shaker with ice and add the vodka, Cointreau, lime juice, and cranberry juice. Shake until cold. Strain into a chilled martini glass, and garnish with the lemon peel.

THE DOS AND DON'TS OF HOSTING A SALON FROM THE DOYENNES OF PARISIAN SALON SOCIETY

The salon was the focal point of Parisian literary society in the twentieth century. Want to recreate the intellectual magic of those resplendent evening hours?

DO FOCUS ON QUALITY

More than just the loyal companion to Gertrude Stein, Alice B. Toklas was a talented cook and consummate entertainer. She took to hosting the many artists and writers that streamed through the front door of 27 rue du Fleurus—including Ernest Hemingway,

Pablo Picasso, F. Scott Fitzgerald, and T. S. Eliot—with artistic flair and philosophical musing:

> Use only the best of everything. If the budget is restricted, restrict the menu to what the budget affords. . . . Your appreciation and appetite will increase. You will add to the pleasure of your guests . . . each morsel must be perfect of its kind, chosen and prepared with love, understanding and erudition.[270]

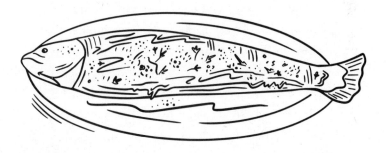

As an epicure and intellectual both, Toklas encountered the finer points of haute cuisine with appreciation and discernment. But she was also playful; her dishes carried poetic, evocative titles and she never eschewed enjoyment. She once served Picasso a fish poached in wine and butter then painted in brightly colored mayonnaises, topped with sieved hard-boiled eggs, truffles, and finely chopped herbs.[271] Delighted as the iconic cubist painter was, he felt the fish more closely alluded to the work of Matisse, and said as much to his hosts.[272] Just like Stein's poetry, Toklas's cooking invited bemusement, bewilderment, and discussion.

DON'T OVERSERVE YOUR GUESTS

Natalie Clifford Barney discouraged the mostly female, mostly queer guests at 20 rue Jacob from drinking during her Friday evening salon.[273] After all, although she welcomed indulgent characters and spirited guests, Barney's salon was a serious endeavor; her Persian-decorated home was a landmark space— one of the first of its kind to celebrate the autonomy of women and elevate the work of lesbian writers.[274] Because of Barney's keen ability to cultivate a lively, diverse, and talented crowd, she didn't have to depend on alcohol to lubricate the evenings. Which is not to say that the nights were dull or deficient. What the evening lacked in libations it gained in company, confections, and the "tinkle of teacups and the chatter."[275] In a biography of Sylvia Beach, proprietor of the Parisian bookstore Shakespeare & Company and attendee of Barney's salons, Noël Riley Fitch describes evenings made sacred by sweets and dance:

Every Friday the famous and eccentric were drawn to her exotic, Persian-decorated rue Jacob rooms. In her garden stood a little temple of Eros, where she and her woman friends danced by moonlight. But during the Friday afternoons of tea and cakes and ices, reputations were launched, diminished, or broken. No alcohol was served by the soft-shoed Chinese servants, but the chocolate cake was from Colombin's and was the best in Paris, Sylvia testifies.[276]

1963

Donna Tartt's
BLACK VELVET

SERVES 1

D onna Tartt, author of *The Secret History* and *The Goldfinch*, swears by the triumvirate of champagne, gin, and whiskey.[277] No surprises there—her aesthetics have been lauded as radically classic and tailored, reflecting her allegiance to that which is timeless and endures. But her style is one of contradictions: she has been described as "friendly but formal," in turns bawdy and coy.[278] Enter the Black Velvet. Like Tartt in a sharp-shouldered velvet blazer, this effervescent mixed drink is slightly bewildering, striking, and a little bit goth (legend holds that this original beer cocktail was served in Great Britain while the kingdom was in mourning for Prince Albert[279]). It's easy to imagine Tartt, a devotee of Irish and British writers, raising a flute to her inspirations: Oscar Wilde, Frank O'Connor, Flann O'Brien and Edna O'Brien, and Charles Dickens.[280]

| 4 ounces champagne | 4 ounces Guinness |

Fill a wine flute halfway with champagne. Top slowly with Guinness.

1964

Bret Easton Ellis's
VODKA AND GRAPEFRUIT JUICE

SERVES 1

This classic bitter combo makes an appearance in several of Ellis's novels, as well as in his memoir *White*. According to an oral history of his alma mater, Bennington College, Ellis once downed multiple vodka grapefruits in rapid succession during a tense hotel-lobby summit with his father;[281] a similarly vodka-laden, tension-ridden hotel lobby scene exists in 1987's *The Rules of Attraction*, and his breakthrough novel *Less Than Zero* makes frequent mention of grapefruit juice and vodka as well.[282] [283] Given art's tendency to imitate life (or vice versa), it's no surprise that debauched scenes populate his works; the frequent use of drugs and alcohol punctuated Ellis's time at Bennington College and at the storied Manhattan nightclubs he presided over as a literary wunderkind afterward.[284]

I found her stillness intimidating, so as a hungover, shaggy twenty-one-year-old I ordered a midday vodka and grapefruit juice to settle my nerves.[285] —*White, 2019*

2 ounces vodka	3 ounces grapefruit juice, freshly squeezed	Lime wedge for garnishing

Pour vodka into a rocks glass. Add ice and grapefruit juice. Garnish with the lime wedge.

1965

J. K. Rowling's
GIN AND TONIC

SERVES 1

J. K. Rowling's fictional universe is steeped not only in potions, but in many delicious and imaginative beverages as well—butterbeer, fire whiskey, and pumpkin juice, to name a few. But Rowling herself prefers a classic from the muggle world: the gin and tonic.[286] Who can fault her? On a summer day, it's magic.

In case you were wondering, this drink is a Slytherin, through and through: strong, slick, and smacks of old money.

I want a large gin.[287] — Excerpt from J. K. Rowling's notebook

2 ounces gin
(Hendrick's)

4 ounces tonic
(Fever-Tree)

Lime wedge
for garnishing

In a collins glass, combine gin and tonic over ice. Garnish with the lime wedge.

Alexander Chee's
PILGRIM AND
NUTTY PINE

 SERVES 1

It was a sort of mixed-up Martinez, with dry vermouth as well as sweet, and a dash of the Peychaud's bitters instead of orange bitters, and a lemon twist, but I liked it so much I made at least two before all was said and done. Meredith noticed and approved after a sip. "I'm on a journey," I said, and she said, "It needs a name," and well, "The Journey" isn't the most auspicious name but maybe "The Pilgrim" is better.[288] —*New York* magazine, 2018

Queen of the Night author Alexander Chee loves gin. He crafted this take on the Martinez, a martini predecessor, one evening at a holiday party in Brooklyn.[289] The Martinez relies on the same skeleton construction as the Manhattan, subbing in gin for whiskey, culling sweetness from vermouth, and drawing complexity from the addition of bitters. Chee's cocktail lacks the saccharine quality that can stifle enjoyment of the Martinez, building off of a Spanish gin, rather than a sweeter Old Tom style, and balancing the sweet vermouth with dry.

PILGRIM

2 ounces gin
(Spanish)

½ ounce dry
vermouth

½ ounce
sweet vermouth

2 dashes
Peychaud's
bitters

Lemon
twist for
garnishing

Combine gin, vermouths, and bitters in a mixing glass filled with ice and stir until chilled. Strain into a chilled coupe glass and garnish with the lemon twist.

NUTTY PINE

The Nutty Pine, Chee's house cocktail for his Catskills home, borrows the basic structure of a Manhattan with the fireside warmth of bourbon and the woodsy, autumnal aromas of pine liqueur and walnut.[290]

---

2 ounces bourbon	2 dashes walnut bitters
½ ounce sweet vermouth	2 dashes pine liqueur

In a mixing glass, combine bourbon, sweet vermouth, bitters, and pine liqueur over ice, and stir until chilled. Strain into a rocks glass over ice, or serve up in a chilled coupe.

1968

Min Jin Lee's
CAMPARI SODA

SERVES 1

Min Jin Lee, the Korean American author of *Free Food for Millionaires* and the 2017 National Book Award finalist *Pachinko*, believes alcohol, like food, "should be consumed with pleasure, gratitude and healthy moderation."[291] Due to her personal history with liver disease, she rarely indulges in spirits. If she does order a cocktail (maybe once in a decade), it will always be a Campari soda—a classic aperitif imbued with bitter citrus notes,[292] and the kind of drink you can linger over in small, contemplative sips.

1 ounce Campari

4 ounces club soda

Orange slice
for garnishing

Pour Campari into a collins glass and add ice. Top with club soda and garnish with the orange slice.

1970 –

Marlon James's
DARK 'N' STORMY

SERVES 1

For Jamaican author and winner of the 2014 Man Booker Prize for *A Brief History of Seven Killings* Marlon James, classic wins out over complicated. "With cocktails," he says, "I prefer if somebody can do a good dark 'n' stormy. One of [the] things I find is everybody spends so much time on fussy cocktails that they screw up the simple ones. And, you'd be amazed how many people screw up a dark 'n' stormy."[293] The dark 'n' stormy, which honors James's Jamaican heritage, depends on the quality of its minimal components, and their proportion. For guidance, just look to the cocktail's name: your rum should be dark and brooding, the ginger beer should be bracing and murky; when you combine them in a highball glass, they should roil against each other, clashing like thunderous clouds and a tumultuous, tropical sea.

2 ounces dark rum
(Gosling's or equivalent
blackstrap)

½ ounce lime juice,
freshly squeezed

4 ounces
ginger beer

Lime wedge
for garnishing

In a highball glass, combine rum and lime juice. Add ice and ginger beer. Garnish with the lime wedge.

PAIR WITH: Curry goat, one of James's favorite traditional Jamaican dishes.

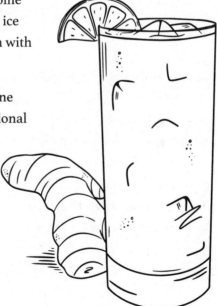

Viet Thanh Nguyen's
SYMPATHIZER

SERVES 1

Pulitzer Prize winner Viet Thanh Nguyen may be a Scotch man himself, but his signature cocktail has a bourbon-laced kick and a celebratory sparkle sure to delight a crowd (filled no doubt with friends, agents-to-be, and artistic rivals).[294] Serve the Sympathizer—which Nguyen details in 2017's *A Literary Cocktail Party*, and which borrows its name from Nguyen's highly acclaimed 2015 novel—at your next book party, award-season fete, or literary luncheon.[295]

¼ ounce bourbon

¼ ounce Aperol

¼ ounce Cynar

¼ ounce lemon juice, freshly squeezed

2 ounces champagne

In a cocktail shaker, combine bourbon, Aperol, Cynar, and lemon juice. Add ice and shake vigorously to combine. Strain into a flute glass, and top with champagne.

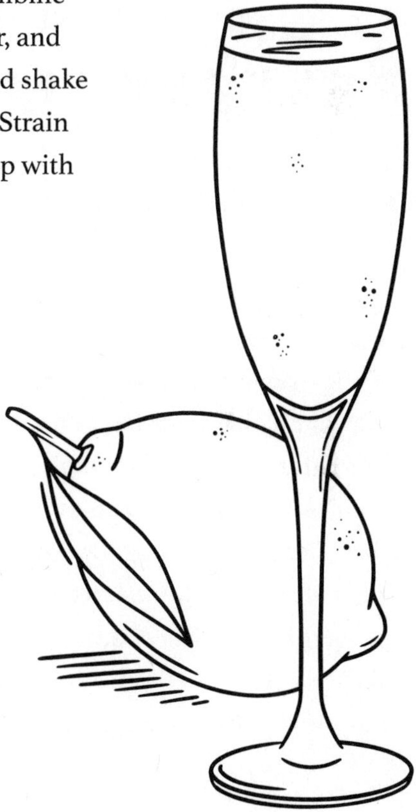

Gary Shteyngart's
BREAKFAST MARTINI*

SERVES 1

The Soviet Union-born, New York-based novelist knows a thing or two about vodka—toasts to good health, good days, bad times, and anything in between are part and parcel of his Russian heritage. Much to the chagrin of purists, his regular order is a vodka tonic.[296] But, like many writers before him, he's known to enjoy a pre-noon martini.[297] And despite his affinity for the Soviet spirit, once in a while he'll spring for gin.[298] His drink of choice at Manhattan's smoked fish and bagel emporium Russ & Daughters has enough protein from egg whites and sweetness from jam to

---

* Adapted from Russ & Daughters

soften the blow from the booze and keep the day open for storyboarding, teaching, and writing countless blurbs for New York's literati.[299]

Absinthe	1 teaspoon strawberry jam	1 dash angostura bitters for garnishing
1 egg white	1 teaspoon simple syrup (1 part sugar dissolved in 1 part water)	
1 ounce gin		
1 ounce lemon juice, freshly squeezed		

Rinse a chilled coupe glass with absinthe. Shake egg white in an empty, chilled cocktail shaker until frothy. Add gin, lemon juice, jam, simple syrup, and ice, and shake vigorously until combined. Strain into the absinthe-rinsed coupe glass. Garnish with the bitters. Enjoy, like Shteyngart, with a plate of pickled herring.

Roxane Gay's
BAD FEMINIST

 SERVES 1

I drank my first drink quickly—a stiff gin and tonic with a splash of grenadine for which Michael teased me mercilessly. "You're basically drinking a Shirley Temple," he said. When I tried to kick him beneath the table, he grabbed my ankle. His hand was warm.[300]
—*An Untamed State*, 2014

R oxane Gay, the Haitian American writer, cultural critic, and author of *Hunger* and *Bad Feminist*, swears by this combination of gin, grenadine, tonic, and lime.[301] Hendrick's, a gin imbued with notes of rose and cucumber, elevates this twist on a classic G&T. Shirley Temple, it is not—especially if you

take the care to make your own grenadine. Drink to take the
edge off the patriarchy.

---

2 ounces
Hendrick's gin

½ ounce grenadine
(see recipe page 103)

½ ounce lime juice,
freshly squeezed

Tonic water

Lime wheel for garnishing

In a mixing glass filled with ice,
combine gin, grenadine, and lime
juice, stirring to combine. Strain
into a collins glass. Add ice and
top with tonic water. Garnish
with the lime wheel.

1975

Taffy Brodesser-Akner's
WHITE RUSSIAN

SERVES 1

Af(fter hunting for her signature drink, the White Russian is where the National Book Award–nominated *Fleishman Is in Trouble* author settled,[302] even if she claims it tastes like "weird milk."[303] And we don't blame her for loving it. There's something comforting and enriching about the Kahlúa-and-vodka concoction. Brodesser-Akner is vegan (save one cheat meal or drink a week)—so we've provided a plant-based version of the classic cocktail that retains all of its trademark creaminess.[304] While the nuttiness of almond milk adds an aromatic dimension to the drink, feel free to experiment with other types of nondairy milk. Or if it's cheat day, heavy cream will work just fine.

1 ½ ounces vodka

¾ ounce Kahlúa

¾ ounce almond milk

In a cocktail shaker filled with ice, combine vodka, Kahlúa, and almond milk. Strain into a rocks glass over ice.

NOTE: When sourcing ingredients, be sure to look for "barista" versions of your nondairy milk, as indicated on the label of the bottle (you can find these at most grocery stores). Because they contain more fat, they are less likely to curdle with other liquids.

Lauren Groff's
DIRTY MARTINI

SERVES 1

R enowned author Lauren Groff—whose books include
Fates and Furies (a favorite of President Barack Obama),
Delicate Edible Birds, and *Florida*—knows that balancing a
writing career and parenthood requires fortitude and efficiency.
In 2017's *A Literary Cocktail Party*, Groff provides her recipe for a
sublimely dirty, bone-dry vodka martini. "I order one of these,"
she writes, "and as soon as I have it in my hand, my whole body
relaxes into the weekend."[305]

2 drops dry vermouth	3 ounces vodka	6 olives for garnishing

Pour vermouth into a chilled martini glass, then shake out. In a cocktail shaker, combine vodka with ice and shake for a very long time. Strain into the martini glass and garnish with 6 olives.

1983

R. O. Kwon's
VODKA SODA

SERVES 1

R. O. Kwon, author of the best-selling *The Incendiaries*, drinks vodka sodas when she's on a book tour.[306] It's the only drink, she claims, that won't leave her hungover.[307] The job of the crisp classic is multiform. It eschews nerves, the ones you might experience before a reading, at the same time that it hydrates. It isn't cloying or complicated, and like a room-service burger, you can count on it in every city.

2 ounces vodka

4 ounces soda water

Lime wedge
for garnishing

Pour vodka over ice into a rocks glass. Top with soda water. Garnish with the lime wedge.

HANGOVER HELP FROM HARD-HITTING, HEDONISTIC, HELL-RAISING WRITERS

In the words of newspaper columnist, film actor, humorist, and member of the Algonquin Round Table Robert Benchley, "the only cure for a real hangover is death."[308] Still, other heavy-drinking writers had their coping mechanisms. After all, between tight deadlines, demanding editors, and shifting economic landscapes, even the most freewheeling authors and poets were forced at some point to buckle down and turn out some pages. The misery-tending that attends merrymaking takes a different form for every writer, though some patterns emerge. Prevention, moderation, and hydration. Just kidding. These writers sought redemption in the hair of the dog, a hit of something salty, a raw egg here and there, and hey, maybe just a splash of laudanum if the doctor saw fit.

ERNEST HEMINGWAY:

Tomato juice and beer.[309]

ZELDA FITZGERALD:

A morning swim followed by a vodka lemonade.[310]

F. SCOTT FITZGERALD:

Three strong whiskies.[311]

P. G. WODEHOUSE:

Worcestershire sauce, raw egg, and red pepper whisked together.

> It is the Worcester sauce that gives it its colour.
> The raw egg makes it nutritious. The red pepper gives it its bite.[312]
> —"Jeeves Takes Charge," 1916

SAMUEL TAYLOR COLERIDGE:

Six fried eggs, a glass of laudanum, and seltzer.[313]

HUNTER S. THOMPSON:

12 amyl nitrates and "as many beers as necessary."[314]

BIBLIOGRAPHY

"10 Things Every True J.K. Rowling Fan Should Know by Now." *Cosmopolitan*, accessed December 10, 2019. https://www.cosmopolitan.com/entertainment/books/a10372546/jk-rowling-facts/.

"About Agatha Christie." The Home of Agatha Christie, accessed December 11, 2019. https://www.agathachristie.com/about-christie.

Acocella, Joan. "A Few Too Many." *New Yorker*, May 19, 2008. https://www.newyorker.com/magazine/2008/05/26/a-few-too-many.

Adams, Jad. *Hideous Absinthe: A History of the Devil in the Bottle*. Madison: University of Wisconsin Press, 2004.

"Alexander Woollcott." *Encyclopaedia Britannica*, accessed December 11, 2019. https://www.britannica.com/biography/Alexander-Woollcott.

"The Algonquin." PUNCH, accessed December 9, 2019. https://punchdrink.com/recipes/algonquin/.

"Algonquin Round Table." *Encyclopaedia Britannica*, accessed November 20, 2019. https://www.britannica.com/biography/ Algonquin-Round-Table.

Allingham, Philip V. "Alcoholic Drink in Charles Dickens's Writing." The Victorian Web, April 24, 2006. http://www.victorianweb.org/ authors/dickens/pva/drink.html.

Amis, Kingsley. *Everyday Drinking: The Distilled Kingsley Amis*. London: Bloomsbury Press, 2009.

Angelou, Maya. "Maya Angelou, The Art of Fiction No. 119." Interview by George Plimpton. *Paris Review* 116, Fall 1990. https://www.theparisreview.org/interviews/2279/ maya-angelou-the-art-of-fiction-no-119-maya-angelou.

Anolik, Lili. "The Secret Oral History of Bennington: The 1980's Most Decadent College." *Esquire*, May 28, 2019. https://www.esquire.com/ entertainment/a27434009/bennington-college-oral-history-bret- easton-ellis/.

Aran, Sue. "Making History: Aromas and Flavors of Past and Present by Alice B. Toklas." Bonjour Paris, December 9, 2015. https://bonjourparis.com/food-and-drink/making-history-aromas-and -flavors-of-past-and-present-by-alice-b-toklas/.

Arata, Emily. "The Surprising Food and Booze Habits of Famous Authors." *First We Feast*, January 4, 2014. https://firstwefeast.com/ drink/2014/01/surprising-food-booze-habits-famous-authors/.

Archibald, Anna. "Scotch, Martinis, and Hard-Boiled Crime: The Life of Dashiell Hammett." Daily Beast, April 4, 2019. https://www.thedailybeast.com/scotch-martinis-and-hard-boiled -crime-the-life-of-dashiell-hammett-author-of-the-big-sleep-and -the-thin-man.

Associated Press. "Poe's Death is Rewritten as a Case of Rabies, Not Telltale Alcohol." *New York Times*, September 15, 1996. https://www.nytimes.com/1996/09/15/us/poe-s-death-is-rewritten-as -case-of-rabies-not-telltale-alcohol.html.

Austen, Jane and J. E. Austen Lee. *A Memoir of Jane Austen.* London: Richard Bentley and Son, 1871.

Avey, Tori. "Eating and Drinking with Charles Dickens." *The History Kitchen*, PBS, December 20, 2012. https://www.pbs.org/food/the -history-kitchen/eating-and-drinking-with-charles-dickens/.

Babitz, Eve. *Sex and Rage.* Counterpoint Press: New York, 2017 (reprint).

Bailey, Mark. *Hemingway & Bailey's Bartending Guide.* New York: Algonquin Books, 2006.

Bainbridge, Julia. "Writer Alexander Chee on Classic Cocktails and What Makes a Good Bartender." Liquor.com, March 11, 2016. https://www.liquor.com/articles/alexander-chee/#gs.lgz4ho.

Barringer, Daisy. "27 San Francisco Cocktails You Need to Drink this Summer." Eventbrite, June 7, 2017. https://www.eventbrite.com/rally/ san-francisco/27-san-francisco-cocktails-need-drink-summer/.

Benfer, Amy. "Gertrude and Alice." Salon, November 18, 1999. https://www.salon.com/1999/11/18/alice/.

"Berlin Station Chief." Mudl Mag, accessed December 16, 2019. http://www.mudlmag.com/berlin-station-chief.

Bicknell, John W., ed. *Selected Letters of Leslie Stephen*. New York: Springer, 1996.

Bieri, James. *Percy Bysshe Shelley: A Biography; Youth's Unextinguished Fire, 1792–1816*. Wilmington: University of Delaware Press, 2004: 357.

Bishop, Elizabeth. *Poems*. New York: Farrar, Strauss and Giroux, 2015.

Black, Alex. "Stirred Not Shaken: Myth-Busting the Martini." Primer, accessed December 9, 2019. https://www.primermagazine.com/2017/learn/stirred-not-shaken-myth-busting-the-martini.

Blinderman, Ilia. "Christopher Hitchens, Who Mixed Drinking & Writing, Names the 'Best Scotch in the History of the World.'" Open Culture, November 18, 2013. http://www.openculture.com/2013/11/christopher-hitchens-names-the-best-scotch-in-the-history-of-the-world.html.

Blinderman, Ilia. "Hunter S. Thompson's Personal Hangover Cure (and the Real Science of Hangovers)." Open Culture, January 18, 2014. http://www.openculture.com/2014/01/hunter-s-thompsons-personal-hangover-cure.html.

Bloom, Howard. *Langston Hughes*. New York: Infobase, 2009.

"Boozy Brunch: The Breakfast Martini." The Shared Sip. April 8, 2016. http://www.thesharedsip.com/boozy-brunch-breakfast-martini/.

Bourdain, Anthony. "Anthony Bourdain Tells Maxim About the Most Dangerous Negroni He's Ever Made." *Maxim*, updated December 18, 2017. https://www.maxim.com/entertainment/anthony-bourdain -tells-maxim-about-most-dangerous-negroni-hes-ever.

Brander, Laurence. "William Makepeace Thackeray." *Encyclopaedia Britannica*, updated November 11, 2019. https://www.britannica.com/ biography/William-Makepeace-Thackeray.

Brodesser-Akner, Taffy and Chris Crowley, ed. "Author Taffy Brodesser-Akner Loves a Good Breakfast Salad." *Grub Street, New York* magazine, June 14, 2019. http://www.grubstreet.com/2019/06/ taffy-brodesser-akner-grub-street-diet.html.

Brouse, Logan R. "Ernest Hemingway's Guide to Tense, Haunting Hangovers." That's, October 19, 2017. https://www.thatsmags.com/ shanghai/post/20993/ernest-hemingway-s-guide-to-an -existential-hangover.

Brouwer, Marilyn. "Zelda Fitzgerald: The Paris Years." Bonjour Paris, April 19, 2018. https://bonjourparis.com/expats-in-paris/zelda- fitzgerald-the-paris-years/.

Bukowski, Charles. *Factotum*. New York: Ecco, 1975.

Bushnell, Candace. *Sex and the City*. New York: Grand Central Publishing, 1996.

Bushnell, Candace. "Swingin' Sex? I Don't Think So . . ." *New York Observer*, April 18, 2007. https://observer.com/2007/04/swingin-sex-i-dont-think-so/.

Burton, Monica. "Why Is So Much Wine Writing Bad?" Eater, September 5, 2017. https://www.eater.com/2017/9/5/16228240/jay-mcinerney-bad-wine-writing-interview.

Butler, Stephanie. "Shakespeare's Suppers." History, January 9, 2019. https://www.history.com/news/shakespeares-suppers.

Cadogan, Mary. "Sloe Gin." BBC Good Food, recipe from *Good Food* magazine, accessed December 11, 2019. https://www.bbcgoodfood.com/recipes/sloe-gin.

"Caipirinha." Liquor.com, accessed December 10, 2019. https://www.liquor.com/recipes/caipirinha/#gs.xbt8pk.

"Caipirinha." PUNCH, accessed December 10, 2019. https://punchdrink.com/recipes/caipirinha/.

Caitlin. "Absinthe, A Conduit to Belle Epoque Paris." *Behind the Bar*, September, 2014. https://www.behindthebar.com/blog/absinthe-belle-epoque-paris/.

Capote, Truman. "New Again: Truman Capote." Interview by Andy Warhol and Bob Colacello. *Interview* magazine, September 16, 2018 (reprint). https://www.interviewmagazine.com/culture/new-again-truman-capote-1.

Capote, Truman. "Truman Capote, The Art of Fiction No. 17."
Interview by Pati Hill. *Paris Review* no. 16, Spring-Summer 1957.
https://www.theparisreview.org/interviews/4867/truman-capote
-the-art-of-fiction-no-17-truman-capote.

Carlson, Jen. "Celebrate NYE with Mark Twain's Favorite Whiskey
Cocktail." Gothamist, December 31, 2013. https://gothamist.com/food/
celebrate-nye-with-mark-twains-favorite-whiskey-cocktail.

Carr, Virginia Spencer. *The Lonely Hunter: A Biography of Carson
McCullers*. Athens, Georgia: University of Georgia Press, 2003.

Carroll, E. Jean. *HUNTER: The Strange and Savage Life of Hunter
S. Thompson*. New York: Dutton, 1993.

Carver, Raymond. "Raymond Carver, The Art of Fiction No. 76."
Interview by Mona Simpson and Lewis Buzbee. *Paris Review* no. 88,
1983. https://www.theparisreview.org/interviews/3059/
raymond-carver-the-art-of-fiction-no-76-raymond-carver.

Cavanaugh, Ray. "The Truncated Drinking Career of America's
Shakespeare: Eugene O'Neill." *Modern Drunkard Magazine*, no. 59,
accessed December 17, 2019. https://drunkard.com/the-truncated
-drinking-career-of-americas-shakespeare-eugene-oneill/.

Cecchini, Toby. "Grenadine Syrup." *New York Times*, accessed
December 9, 2019. https://cooking.nytimes.com/recipes/1015334
-grenadine-syrup.

Celli, Robert. "Vesuvio Café." *The Semaphore* 186, Winter 2009.
http://www.foundsf.org/index.php?title=Vesuvio_Caf%C3%A9.

"Celtic Druid's Honey Mead - Meade - Metheglin." Recipes /
Beverages, *Food*, accessed December 10, 2019. https://www.food.com/
recipe/celtic-druids-honey-mead-meade-metheglin-216215.

Chandler, Raymond. *The Long Goodbye*. New York: Houghton Mifflin
Harcourt, 1953.

"Charles Bukowski." *Encyclopaedia Britannica*, updated December 12,
2019. https://www.britannica.com/biography/Charles-Bukowski.

"Charles Bukowski," Poet's Graves, accessed December 21, 2019.
https://www.poetsgraves.co.uk/bukowski.htm.

Chee, Alexander and Chris Crowley, ed. "Author Alexander Chee
Pairs *The Great British Baking Show* with Vodka Martinis." *Grub Street*,
New York magazine, December 21, 2018. http://www.grubstreet.
com/2018/12/alexander-chee-grub-street-diet.html.

Chee, Alexander. "The Poisoning." *Tin House* no. 72, July 25, 2017.
https://tinhouse.com/the-poisoning/.

Cheh, Carol. "Looking at Los Angeles: In Search of Eve Babitz."
Art21, May 25, 2012. https://magazine.art21.org/2012/05/25/looking-at
-los-angeles-in-search-of-eve-babitz/#.Xe-1adVKGgR.

Chilton, Martin. "The Odd Life of *Catcher in the Rye* Author JD Salinger." *Independent*, January 1, 2019. https://www.independent.co.uk/arts-entertainment/books/features/jd-salinger-life-catcher-in-rye-books-anniversary-franny-zooey-raise-high-roof-beam-john-lennon-a8699026.html.

"Chloral Hydrate Capsule." Drugs & Medication, WebMD, accessed December 16, 2019. https://www.webmd.com/drugs/2/drug-8629/chloral-hydrate-oral/details.

"The Christopher Hitchens Guide to Drinking (for the Young) and Artistically Minded." FreshlyWorded, August 2, 2013. https://freshlyworded.com/2013/08/02/the-christopher-hitchens-guide-to-drinking-for-the-young-and-artistically-minded/.

"The Chumleys." Researching Greenwich Village History, November 5, 2010. https://greenwichvillagehistory.wordpress.com/2010/11/05/the-chumleys/.

Ciabattari, Jane. "Absinthe: How the Green Fairy Became Literature's Drink." Culture, BBC, January 9, 2014. http://www.bbc.com/culture/story/20140109-absinthe-a-literary-muse/.

Clarke, Paul. "El Floridita Daiquiri Recipe." Serious Eats, June 11, 2010. https://www.seriouseats.com/recipes/2010/06/el-floridita-daiquiri-drink-cocktail-recipe.html.

Clarke, Paul. "Pisco Sour Recipe." Serious Eats, February 11, 2019. https://www.seriouseats.com/recipes/2011/02/time-for-a-drink-pisco-sour.html.

Cleary, Skye C. "New York Cocktail Philosophy." Huffington Post, July 19, 2016. https://www.huffpost.com/entry/new-york-cocktail -philoso_b_7827076.

Cline, Sally. *Zelda Fitzgerald: Her Voice in Paradise*. New York: Arcade Publishing, 2003.

Clough, David. "Celebrity Drinks: The Favorite Drinks of 14 Famous New Yorkers." Culture, The Drink Nation, June 16, 2013. https://thedrinknation.com/articles/read/10857-Celebrity-Drinks-The -Favorite-Drinks-of-14-Famous-New-Yorkers#.

"Clover Club." PUNCH, accessed December 10, 2019. https://punchdrink.com/recipes/clover-club/.

"Cocktail Hour: Drink What Charles Dickens Drank." Four Pounds Flour: Historic Gastronomy. October 29, 2010. http://www.fourpoundsflour.com/cocktail-hour-drink-what-dickens -drank/.

"The Cocktail Hour: Carson McCullers." Paper and Salt, October 4, 2013. https://paperandsalt.org/2013/10/04/the-cocktail-hour-carson -mccullers/.

"The Cocktail Hour: E. B. White's Martini." Paper and Salt, March 8, 2012. https://paperandsalt.org/2012/03/08/the-cocktail-hour-e-b-white/.

"The Cocktail Hour: Edgar Allan Poe." Paper and Salt, January 7, 2013. https://paperandsalt.org/2013/01/07/the-cocktail-hour-edgar -allan-poe/.

"The Cocktail Hour: Evelyn Waugh." Paper and Salt, December 8, 2014. https://paperandsalt.org/2014/12/08/the-cocktail-hour-evelyn-waugh/.

"The Cocktail Hour: Raymond Carver." Paper and Salt, June 7, 2014. https://paperandsalt.org/2014/07/07/bloody-mary-cocktail-raymond-carver/.

Coetzee, J. M. "The Razor's Edge." *New York Review of Books*, November 1, 2001. https://www.nybooks.com/articles/2001/11/01/the-razors-edge.

Coffey, Edel. "Interview: The Very, Very Private Life of Ms. Donna Tartt." *Independent*, November 26, 2013. https://www.independent.ie/lifestyle/interview-the-very-very-private-life-of-ms-donna-tartt-29780543.html.

Collins, Amy Fine. "Once Was Never Enough." *Vanity Fair*, August 26, 2013. https://www.vanityfair.com/culture/2000/01/jacqueline-susann-valley-of-the-dolls-books.

Collins, Jackie. *The Lucky Santangelo Cookbook*. New York: St. Martin's Press, 2014.

Compagno, Natalie. "Murder, Gin, and the Queen of Crime: Agatha Christie's Devon & Cornwall." Huffington Post, August 4, 2015. https://www.huffpost.com/entry/devon-cornwall_b_7930480.

"Cosmopolitan: Toby Cecchini." PUNCH, accessed December 9, 2019. https://punchdrink.com/recipes/cosmopolitan/.

Coward, Noël. *Relative Values: A Light Comedy in Three Acts*. New York: Samuel French, 1952.

Crosariol, Beppi. "A Gin Toast to Dickens with a Twist." *Globe and Mail*, December 24, 2014. https://www.theglobeandmail.com/life/food-and-wine/recipes/a-gin-toast-to-dickens-with-a-twist/article22179475/.

Curran, John. "She Never Went to School: 126 Remarkable Agatha Christie Facts." *Irish Times*, October 10, 2016. https://www.irishtimes.com/culture/books/she-never-went-to-school-126-remarkable-agatha-christie-facts-1.2820918.

Dalkin, Gaby. "Pisco Sour." What's Gaby Cooking, October 28, 2013. https://whatsgabycooking.com/pisco-sour/.

Damuck, Jessie. "New-New Bloody Mary." *Bon Appetit*, accessed January 7, 2020. https://www.bonappetit.com/recipe/new-new-bloody-mary.

Dangremond, Sam. "How to Make F. Scott Fitzgerald's Favorite Cocktail: The Gin Rickey." *Town & Country*, August 10, 2018. https://www.townandcountrymag.com/leisure/drinks/a1549/f-scott-fitzgerald-gin-rickey-cocktail/.

"Dante Gabriel Rossetti." The Poetry Foundation, accessed December 16, 2019. https://www.poetryfoundation.org/poets/dante-gabriel-rossetti.

Davis, T. Wylie. "Chile." *Sun Sentinel*, March 7, 1999. https://www.sun-sentinel.com/news/fl-xpm-1999-03-07 -9903020997-story.html.

Demarest, Rebecca A. "C'est Moi: Gustave Flaubert's 'Madame Bovary.'" *Inquiries Journal* 3 no. 3, 2011.

Denig, Vicki. "The Classic Kir." *Wine Enthusiast*, March 15, 2018. https://www.winemag.com/recipe/the-classic-kir-cocktail/.

Dent, Bryan. "Under the Influence: Charles Bukowski, High Laureate of Cheap Booze." *Modern Drunkard Magazine* no. 62, accessed December 17, 2019. https://drunkard.com/under-the-influence -charles-bukowski-high-laureate-of-cheap-booze/.

Derk, Peter. "Flannery O'Connor's Greatest Hits." Lit Reactor, March 23, 2018. https://litreactor.com/columns/flannery-oconnors -greatest-hits.

Dibblee, Tom. "Jay McInerney, The New York Fantasy, and Wine." *Los Angeles Review of Books*, October 3, 2012. https://lareviewofbooks.org/ article/jay-mcinerney-the-new-york-fantasy-and-wine/.

Dorgan, Michael. "Bloomsday: The Meals James Joyce Would Have Enjoyed." Irish Central, June 16, 2019. https://www.irishcentral.com/ culture/food-drink/bloomsday-the-meals-james-joyce-would -have-enjoyed.

Doyle, Jessica. "Cocktails in Literature." AbeBooks, accessed December 16, 2019. https://www.abebooks.com/books/rarebooks/ vintage-cocktail-books/cocktails-in-literature.shtml.

Dubow, Charles. "Hangover Cures." *Forbes*, January 1, 2004. https://www.forbes.com/2003/01/01/cx_cd_0101featsidebar. html#49f78cc44d77.

Dunn, Elizabeth G. "The Kir Cocktail Is Cool Again." *Wall Street Journal*, August 19, 2015. https://www.wsj.com/articles/ the-kir-cocktail-is-cool-again-1440011729.

Dyke, SC. "Some Medical Aspects of the Life of Dante Gabriel Rossetti." *Proceedings of the Royal Society of Medicine* 56 (December 1963): 39–43. https://journals.sagepub.com/doi/pdf/10.1177/ 003591576305601218.

"Edgar Rice Burroughs." *Encyclopaedia Britannica*, accessed December 11, 2019. https://www.britannica.com/biography/Edgar-Rice-Burroughs.

"El Coquetelon." Wayfaring Seels, December 17, 2014. http://www.wayfaringseels.com/global-spirits/el-coquetelon-pablo -nerudas-specialty-cocktail.

Ellis, Bret Easton. *Less Than Zero*. New York: Simon & Schuster, 1985.

Ellis, Bret Easton. *The Rules of Attraction*. New York: Simon & Schuster, 1987.

Ellis, Bret Easton. *White*. New York: Alfred A. Knopf, 2019.

Emeott, Donna Michael. "Edgar Allan Poe's Family Eggnog Recipe." The Family Cookbook Project, accessed November 20, 2019. https://www.familycookbookproject.com/recipe/3612329/edgar -allan-poes-family-eggnog.html.

English, Camper. "The Key to Crystal-Clear Cocktails? Milk. (Really.)" *Cooks Illustrated*, December 4, 2016. https://www.cooksillustrated.com/ science/844-articles/story/the-key-to-crystal-clear-cocktails -milk-really.

Erlich, Jessica Prince. "How I Get It Done: *Sex and the City* Author Candace Bushnell." *The Cut, New York* magazine, February 15, 2019. https://www.thecut.com/2019/02/sex-and-the-city-candace-bushnell -on-life-after-50.html.

"Eudora Welty." *Encyclopaedia Britannica,* updated July 30, 2019, https://www.britannica.com/biography/Eudora-Welty.

"Eudora Welty's White Fruit Cake." *Cooking Bride*, accessed December 16, 2019. https://cookingbride.com/desserts/cakes/white-fruitcake/.

Fanelli, Brian. "He Too Sings America: Jazz, Laughter, and Sound as Protest in Langston Hughes's Harlem." The The Poetry, August 18, 2014. https://www.thethepoetry.com/2014/08/he-too-sings-america -jazz-laughter-and-sound-as-protest-in-langston-hughess-harlem.

Farley, John. *The London Art of Cookery and Housekeeper's Complete Assistant on a New Plan*. Dublin: Price, Sleater, Lynch, Whitestone, Burnet, Walker, White, Moncrieffe, Beatty, Burton, Byrne, Perrin, and Cash, 1783.

Feddersen, Matthew. "From Australia With Love: Pretty Boys Don't Buy Their Own Drinks." *TWELV Mag*, August 23, 2013. https://twelvmag.com/people/australia-love-pretty-boys-dont-buy-their-own-drinks?page=6.

Felten, Eric. "Less Sugar, More Sting." *Wall Street Journal*, November 3, 2007. https://www.wsj.com/articles/SB119403314575880733.

Fitch, Noel Riley. *Sylvia Beach and the Lost Generation: A History of Paris in the Twenties and Thirties*. New York: W.W. Norton, 1985.

Fitzgerald, Helena. "Drinking With Novelist Gary Shteyngart." PUNCH, September 4, 2018. https://punchdrink.com/articles/drinking-with-absurdistan-author-gary-shteyngart/.

FitzSimons, Marinel. "The Top 10 Literary Drinks." The Drinks Business, August 26, 2011. https://www.thedrinksbusiness.com/2011/08/the-top-10-literary-drinks/10/.

Fleming, Anne Taylor. "The Private World of Truman Capote." *New York Times*, July 9, 1978. https://www.nytimes.com/1978/07/09/archives/the-private-world-of-truman-capote.html.

Fleming, Ian. *Casino Royale*. London: J. Cape, 1953.

Flynn, Katherine. "New York City's White Horse Tavern." National Trust for Historic Preservation, March 6, 2015. https://www.savingplaces.org/stories/historic-bars-new-york -citys-white-horse-tavern#.Xf52gtVKGgQ.

Foley, Meghan. "Here's How to Drink Absinthe Like Hemingway and Van Gogh." Showbiz Cheatsheet, May 30, 2017. https://www.cheatsheet.com/culture/heres-how-to-drink-absinthe- like-hemingway-and-van-gogh.html/.

Garner, Dwight. "Lawrence Ferlinghetti's Enduring San Francisco." *New York Times*, March 11, 2019. https://www.nytimes.com/2019/03/11/ travel/lawrence-ferlinghettis-enduring-san-francisco.html.

Garret, Dylan. "The Jack Rose Cocktail, a True American Classic." *Wine Enthusiast*, July 6, 2019. https://www.winemag.com/recipe/ jack-rose-cocktail/.

Garret, Dylan. "The Story (and Recipe) Behind the Hemingway Daiquiri." *Wine Enthusiast*, July 21, 2017. https://www.winemag.com/ recipe/the-story-and-recipe-behind-the-hemingway-daiquiri/.

Gay, Roxane. *An Untamed State*. New York: Grove Atlantic, 2014.

Gelb, Arthur and Barbara Gelb. "Eugene O'Neill." *Encyclopaedia Britannica*, updated October 12, 2019. https://www.britannica.com/ biography/Eugene-ONeill.

"George Orwell - A Nice Strong Cuppa and a Pint of Mild." Lovely Linda Loves Life, March 18, 2019. http://lovelylindaloveslife. blogspot.com/2019/03/george-orwell-nice-strong-cuppa-and.html.

"Gertrude Stein and Alice B. Toklas: Summer Champagne Fruit Salad." Paper and Salt, June 29, 2017. https://paperandsalt.org/ 2017/06/29/gertrude-stein-summer-champagne-fruit-salad/.

"Gin Rickey." PUNCH, accessed December 9, 2019. https://punchdrink.com/recipes/gin-rickey/.

"Gin Twist." Difford's Guide, accessed December 16, 2019. https://www.diffordsguide.com/cocktails/recipe/2934/gin-twist.

Godwin, Richard. *The Spirits*. New York: Penguin Random House, 2015.

The Good Life France. "Normandy Hot Toddy." The Good Life France, accessed December 16, 2019. https://www.thegoodlifefrance. com/normandy-hot-toddy/.

Gopnik, Adam. "Writers and Rum." *New Yorker*, January 9, 2014. https://www.newyorker.com/books/page-turner/writers-and-rum.

Graham, Colleen. "Between the Sheets Cocktail Recipe." The Spruce Eats, August 7, 2019. https://www.thespruceeats.com/ between-the-sheets-cocktail-recipe-759286.

Graham, Colleen. "Black Velvet Cocktail." The Spruce Eats, August 8, 2019. https://www.thespruceeats.com/black-velvet-recipe-759594.

Graham, Colleen. "James Bond's Famous Vesper Martini." The Spruce Eats, May 20, 2019. https://www.thespruceeats.com/vesper-martini-recipe-760130.

Greenberg, Arnie. "Natalie Clifford Barney: Host of Left Bank Literary Salons." Bonjour Paris, May 11, 2005. https://bonjourparis.com/archives/natalie-clifford-barney-left-bank-literary/.

Greene, Philip. "The Myth Behind Hemingway's Favorite Drink." Eater, December 9, 2015. https://www.eater.com/drinks/2015/12/9/9880450/hemingway-mojito-havana-myth.

Greg. "19th Century Poet Lord Byron Had a Wine Goblet That Was Made Out of a Human Skull." Daily Grail, October 4, 2017. https://www.dailygrail.com/2017/10/19th-century-poet-lord-byron-had-a-wine-goblet-that-was-made-out-of-a-human-skull/.

Guthmann, Edward. "Jackson, Miss., Celebrates Author Eudora Welty." *SFGate*, March 29, 2019. https://www.sfgate.com/travel/article/Jackson-Miss-celebrates-author-Eudora-Welty-3246701.php.

"Gwendolyn Bennett." My Black History, accessed December 17, 2019. https://www.myblackhistory.net/Gwendolyn_Bennett.htm.

Halliday, Ayun. "Eudora Welty's Handwritten Eggnog Recipe and Charles Dickens' Recipe for Holiday Punch." Open Culture, December 22, 2017. http://www.openculture.com/2017/12/eudora-weltys-handwritten-eggnog-recipe-and-charles-dickens-recipe-for-holiday-punch.html.

Hammonds, Karen. "Milk Punch." Revolutionary Pie, July 18, 2016. https://revolutionarypie.com/2016/07/18/milk-punch/.

"Hangman's Blood." CocktailBook, accessed December 21, 2019. https://www.cocktailbook.com/hangmans-blood/.

Heaney, Seamus. "Sloe Gin." *Station Island*. London: Faber and Faber, 1984.

Hémard, Ned. "Milk with a Punch." New Orleans Nostalgia, New Orleans Bar Association, 2010, accessed December 17, 2019. https://www.neworleansbar.org/uploads/files/MilkwithaPunchArticle212-1.pdf.

Hernandez, Pilar. "Completos or Chilean Hot Dogs." Pilar's Chilean Food & Garden, June 4, 2009. https://www.chileanfoodandgarden.com/chilean-completos-or-hot-dogs/.

Hiatt, Fred. "Haruki Murakami's Homecoming." *Washington Post*, December 25, 1989. https://www.washingtonpost.com/archive/lifestyle/1989/12/25/haruki-murakamis-homecoming/b62514a4-6f77-473c-b3a9-75b00b2a41ba/.

Hicks, Jesse. "The Devil in a Little Green Bottle: A History of Absinthe." Distillations, Science History Institute, October 4, 2010. https://www.sciencehistory.org/distillations/the-devil-in-a-little-green-bottle-a-history-of-absinthe.

Higgins, Chris. "George Orwell's 11 Tips for Proper Tea Making." Mental Floss, January 21, 2018. https://www.mentalfloss.com/article/73943/george-orwells-11-tips-proper-tea-making.

Higgins, Will. "Bourbon in the P.M. with James Baldwin." *IndyStar*, February 13, 2017. https://www.indystar.com/story/life/2017/02/13/bourbon-pm-james-baldwin/97602100/.

Hitchens, Christopher. "Living Proof." *Vanity Fair*, March 16, 2003. https://www.vanityfair.com/news/2003/03/hitchens-200303.

"Horse's Neck." PUNCH, accessed December 16, 2019. https://punchdrink.com/recipes/horses-neck/.

"How Art Girls Cure Their Hangovers." TheArtGorgeous, March 6, 2019. https://theartgorgeous.com/hangover-cures-art-world/.

Howe, Holly. "9 TOP Fermentation Lids for Mason Jar Fermentation [HOW AIRLOCKS WORK]." *MakeSauerkraut!,* May 4, 2017. https://www.makesauerkraut.com/fermentation-lids/.

Hughes, Emma. "How to Cure a Hangover, by Some of Britain's Greatest Writers." *Country Life*, January 1, 2018. https://www.countrylife.co.uk/food-drink/literary-hangover-cures-67593.

Hughes, Langston. *The Big Sea: An Autobiography*. New York: Farrar, Straus and Giroux, 2015.

Hughes, Richard. *A High Wind in Jamaica*. New York: New York Review of Books, 1999.

"Hunter S. Thompson." *Encyclopaedia Britannica*, last updated November 20, 2019. https://www.britannica.com/biography/ Hunter-S-Thompson#ref837474.

Hurst, D. L. and M. J. Hurst. "Bromide psychosis: a literary case." *Clin Nueropharmacol* 7, no. 3 (1984): 259–264.

Imbibe staff. "Corpse Reviver #2." Imbibe, October 24, 2019. https://imbibemagazine.com/corpse-reviver-2-recipe/.

Imbibe staff. "Holy Joe Cocktail." Imbibe, December 29, 2016. https://imbibemagazine.com/holy-joe-cocktail/.

"Jackie Collins," *Encyclopaedia Britannica,* accessed December 21, 2019. https://www.britannica.com/biography/Jackie-Collins.

James, Marlon and Chris Crowley, ed. "Author Marlon James Has No Time for Fussy Cocktails." *Grub Street, New York* magazine, March 22, 2019. http://www.grubstreet.com/2019/03/marlon-james-grub -street-diet.html.

"John Steinbeck." *Encyclopaedia Britannica*, accessed December 20, 2019. https://www.britannica.com/biography/John-Steinbeck.

Jones, Carey and John D. McCarthy. "3 Quick Cocktails Starring Sloe Gin." *Food & Wine*, June 22, 2017. https://www.foodandwine.com/fwx/ drink/3-quick-cocktails-starring-sloe-gin.

Jones, Nicole. "To Eve Babitz, Who Wrote the Best Dedication Page in All of Literature." *Vanity Fair*, September 29, 2015. https://www.vanityfair.com/culture/2015/09/eve-babitz-wrote-best-dedication-page-in-literature.

Joyce, James. *Dubliners*. New York: Penguin, 2007.

Kamholz, Roger. "Is There a Better Way to Make a Martini?" PUNCH, January 20, 2017. https://punchdrink.com/articles/is-there-a-better-way-to-make-a-martini-cocktail-recipe/.

Kaplan, James. "Smart Tartt." *Vanity Fair*, September 1999. https://www.vanityfair.com/news/1992/09/donna-tartt-the-secret-history.

Katherine Anne Porter Correspondence Project. "About Katherine Anne Porter." University Libraries, University of Maryland, accessed December 18, 2019, https://www.lib.umd.edu/kaporter-correspondence/about-kaporter.

"Katherine Anne Porter." *Encyclopaedia Britannica*, updated September 14, 2019. https://www.britannica.com/biography/Katherine-Anne-Porter.

Katrandjian, Olivia. "Pablo Neruda's Chile: Where Oddities and Inspirations Abound." Huffington Post, December 6, 2017. https://www.huffpost.com/entry/pablo-neruda-chile_b_958606.

Kealy, R. M. "Writer's Tipples: 'The Screwdriver' Recipe—Truman Capote." R.M. Kealy, accessed December 10, 2019. http://www.rmkealy.com/2014/02/04/writers-tipples-screwdriver-truman-capote/.

Kealy, R. M. "Writers' Tipples: Whiskey Sour Recipe—Dorothy Parker." R.M. Kealy, accessed November 20, 2019. http://www.rmkealy.com/2014/03/09/writers-tipples-whiskey-sour-recipe-dorothy-parker/.

Kendrick, Julie. "I'm Never Drinking Again: The Science Behind Hangovers." Growler, June 26, 2017. https://growlermag.com/science-behind-hangovers/2/.

Killius, Jen. "The Clover Club: Philly's Original Cocktail." *Drink Philly*, October 14, 2011. https://philly.thedrinknation.com/articles/read/5731-The-Clover-Club-Phillys-Original-Cocktail#.

King, Kara. "Anthony Bourdain Reveals His 'Perfect Drink.'" Thrillist, April 8, 2016. https://www.thrillist.com/news/nation/anthony-bourdains-favorite-drinks.

King, Steven. "Raymond Carver's Life and Stories." *New York Times*, November 19, 2009.

Knower, Rosemary. "An Alice B. Toklas Celebration of the End of Summer." *Baltimore Sun*, September 23, 1990. https://www.baltimoresun.com/news/bs-xpm-1990-09-23-1990266099-story.html.

Kost, Ryan. "Vesuvio Cafe, Habitat of San Francisco's Beatniks, Celebrates 70 Years." *Datebook*, September 25, 2018. https://datebook.sfchronicle.com/entertainment/vesuvio-cafe-home -to-the-beatniks-celebrates-70-years.

Kress, Nancy. *Write Great Fiction: Characters, Emotion & Viewpoint.* New York: Penguin, 2005.

Kubala, Jillian. "7 Benefits and Uses of CBD Oil (Plus Side Effects)," Healthline, February 26, 2018. https://www.healthline.com/nutrition/ cbd-oil-benefits.

"Kummel–Calming Those First-Tee Nerves." The Whisky Exchange, July 17, 2014. https://www.blog.thewhiskyexchange.com/2014/07/ kummel/.

Kwon, R. O. and Chris Crowley, ed. "Author R. O. Kwon Spends Her Day Off with Tacos." *Grub Street, New York* magazine, August 10, 2018. http://www.grubstreet.com/2018/08/author-r-o-kwon-grub-street -diet.html.

"La Bodeguita del Medio Original Mojito Recipe." Findery, accessed December 10, 2019. https://findery.com/eolmosc2/notes/la-bodeguita -del-medio-original-mojito-recipe.

Laing, Olivia. "'Every Hour a Glass of Wine' – The Female Writers Who Drank." *The Guardian*, June 13, 2014. https://www.theguardian. com/books/2014/jun/13/alcoholic-female-women-writers-marguerite -duras-jean-rhys.

Laing, Olivia. "What Would Britain Be Without Drink?" *The Guardian*, January 9, 2016. https://www.theguardian.com/commentisfree/2016/jan/10/alcohol-guidelines-drinking-orwell-perfect-pub.

Lanahan, Eleanor. "Behind the Myths of Scott and Zelda's Epic Romance." Literary Hub, July 23, 2019. https://lithub.com/behind-the-myths-of-scott-and-zeldas-epic-romance/.

Lawrence, Doc. "Gourmet Highway: Zelda, Angel from Alabama." *My Cooking Magazine*, accessed December 16, 2019. https://www.mycookingmagazine.com/gourmet-highway-zelda-angel-from-alabama/.

Leasca, Stacey. "Anthony Bourdain is Making This Cocktail Popular Again." *Travel + Leisure*, July 14, 2017. https://www.travelandleisure.com/food-drink/celebrity-chefs/anthony-bourdain-negronis.

Lee, Ann. "JK Rowling Unveils New Website and Immediately Demands 'Large Gin.'" *Metro*, December 21, 2016. https://metro.co.uk/2016/12/21/jk-rowling-unveils-new-website-and-immediately-talks-about-gin-6337905/.

Lee, Min Jin. "Interview with Min Jin Lee, Author of 'Free Food for Millionaires,'" interview by Caren, *Drinking Diaries from Celebration to Revelation*, August 10, 2011. https://www.drinkingdiaries.com/2011/08/10/interview-with-min-jin-lee/.

"Lifestyle and Legacy of the Bloomsbury Group." Art & Artists, Tate Museum, accessed December 16, 2019. https://www.tate.org.uk/art/art-terms/b/bloomsbury/lifestyle-lives-and-legacy-bloomsbury-group.

Lyon, Shauna. "The Rich Literary History of Chumley's." *New Yorker*, December 8, 2016. https://www.newyorker.com/magazine/2016/12/19/the-rich-literary-history-of-chumleys.

Mabillard, Amanda. "Shakespeare's Drinking." Shakespeare Online, August 20, 2000. http://www.shakespeare-online.com/faq/shakespearedrinking.html.

"The Magic Island." *Encyclopaedia Britannica*, accessed December 11, 2019. https://www.britannica.com/topic/The-Magic-Island.

Mailer, Norman. *Harlot's Ghost: A Novel*. New York: Random House, 2007.

"Making Sloe Gin Part 1: Hunting for Sloes." Gin Foundry, November 9, 2018. https://www.ginfoundry.com/insights/making-sloe-gin-part-1-hunting-for-sloes/.

Malcolm, Janet. "The Odd Couple." *The Guardian*, October 26, 2007. https://www.theguardian.com/books/2007/oct/27/featuresreviews.guardianreview31.

"Manhattan." PUNCH, accessed December 16, 2019. https://punchdrink.com/recipes/manhattan/.

"Margarita." PUNCH, accessed December 9, 2019. https://punchdrink.com/recipes/margarita/.

Markel, Dr. Howard. "F. Scott Fitzgerald's Life Was a Study in Destructive Alcoholism." PBS, April 11, 2017. https://www.pbs.org/newshour/health/f-scott-fitzgeralds-life-study-destructive-alcoholism.

Marks, Arley. "A Wheatgrass Margarita for the Sanctimonious Lush." *Vanity Fair*, June 6, 2015. https://www.vanityfair.com/culture/2015/06/dimes-wheatgrass-margarita-arley-marks-recipe.

"Mark Twain." Cocktailia, December 30, 2007. https://www.cocktailia.com/cocktail-recipes/mark-twain/.

"Martinez." PUNCH, accessed December 9, 2019. https://punchdrink.com/recipes/martinez/.

Marrs, Suzanne. *Eudora Welty: A Biography*. New York: Houghton Mifflin Harcourt, 2015.

Marrus, Michael R. "Social Drinking in the Belle Epoque." *Journal of Social History* 7, no. 2 (Winter, 1974): 115–141. https://www.jstor.org/stable/3786351?seq=1.

Martyris, Nina. "Collards and Canoodling: How Helen Gurley Brown Promoted Premarital Cooking," The Salt, NPR, July 26, 2016. https://www.npr.org/sections/thesalt/2016/07/26/486803177/collards-and-canoodling-how-helen-gurley-brown-promoted-premarital-cooking.

Martyris, Nina. "How Percy Shelley Stirred His Politics Into His Tea Cup." The Salt, NPR, August 4, 2015. https://www.npr.org/sections/thesalt/2015/08/04/429363868/how-percy-shelley-stirred-his-politics-into-his-tea-cup.

Maryanski, Maureen. "The Aristocrat of Harlem: The Cotton Club." New York Historical Society, February 17, 2016. http://blog.nyhistory.org/the-aristocrat-of-harlem-the-cotton-club/.

"Maya Angelou." *Encyclopaedia Britannica*, last updated August 2, 2019. https://www.britannica.com/biography/Maya-Angelou.

Maynard, Nora. "Straight Up: Thirsty Reads from Haruki Murakami." Kitchn, March 21, 2008. https://www.thekitchn.com/straight-up-thirsty-reading-fr-45611.

Mazan, Grant. "Kerouac's Margarita," Jet Fuel Review Blog, Lewis Lit Journal, November 17, 2014. https://www.lewislitjournal.wordpress.com/2014/11/17/kerouacs-margarita/.

McAlpine, Fraser. "Five Victorian Cocktails (Including the 'Cock Tail')." BBC America, 2013, accessed December 19, 2019. http://www.bbcamerica.com/anglophenia/2013/06/five-victorian-cocktails-including-the-cock-tail.

McInerney, Jay. "Good Wine and Fax Machines Brought Jay McInerney and Julian Barnes Together." *Town & Country*, August 17, 2017. https://www.townandcountrymag.com/leisure/drinks/a10364108/argument-for-letter-writing/.

McInerney, Jay. "How Jay McInerney Combined His Love of Writing and Wine." *Town & Country*, July 12, 2016. https://www.townandcountrymag.com/society/tradition/news/a6695/ jay-mcinerney-wine-writing/.

Mejia, Paula. "A Brief History of the White Horse Tavern, NYC's Legendary Literary Watering Hole." Gothamist, March 12, 2019. https://www.gothamist.com/food/a-brief-history-of-the-white-horse -tavern-nycs-legendary-literary-watering-hole.

Mickelbart, Stacey. "Joan Didion On Stage." *New Yorker*, November 22, 2011. https://www.newyorker.com/books/page-turner/joan-didion -on-stage.

Monteiro, George. *Elizabeth Bishop in Brazil and After: A Poetic Career Transformed*. North Carolina: McFarland Publishing, 2012.

Montgomery, David J. "Worlds Collide: Raymond Chandler and the Gimlet." Professor Cocktail, October 17, 2011. https://professorcocktail.com/2011/10/17/raymond-chandler-and -the-gimlet/.

Moor, Robert. "Faulkner's Cocktail of Choice." *Paris Review*, December 31, 2013. https://www.theparisreview.org/blog/2013/12/31/ faulkners-cocktail-of-choice/.

Morris, Rob. "Algonquin Round Table." *Oxford Research Encyclopedias*, July 2017. https://oxfordre.com/literature/abstract/10.1093/ acrefore/9780190201098.001.0001/acrefore-9780190201098-e-655.

Munro, Lizzie. "Mastering the Cosmopolitan with Toby Cecchini." PUNCH, June 5, 2017. https://punchdrink.com/articles/how-to -cosmopolitan-cocktail-recipe-toby-cecchini/.

Murakami, Haruki. *Hard-Boiled Wonderland and the End of the World*. New York: Knopf Doubleday Publishing Group, 2011.

Nastasi, Alison. "12 Hangover Cures from the Boozy and Famous." FlavorWire, December 19, 2011. https://www.flavorwire.com/ 242895/12-hangover-cures-from-the-boozy-and-famous.

"Natalie Barney." Elizabeth A. Sackler Center for Feminist Art, Brooklyn Museum, accessed December 17, 2019. https://www.brooklynmuseum.org/eascfa/dinner_party/ place_settings/natalie_barney.

"Negus." The Jane Austen Centre, June 17, 2011. https://www.janeausten.co.uk/negus/.

"Negus from the Mansfield Park Ball." Parbake & Prose, January 19, 2018. https://parbakeandprose.com/2018/01/19/ negus-mansfield-park-ball/.

"Noël Coward." *Encyclopaedia Britannica*, last updated December 12, 2019. https://www.britannica.com/biography/Noel-Coward.

"Norman Mailer." *Encyclopaedia Britannica*, last upated November 6, 2019. https://www.britannica.com/biography/Norman-Mailer.

Norris, Michael. "A Drink of Absinthe." Literary Kicks, February 14, 2008. https://www.litkicks.com/ADrinkOfAbsinthe.

North, Sterling and Carl Kroch. *So Red the Nose or—Breath in the Afternoon*. New York: Farrar & Rinehart, 1935.

Nurin, Tara. "The Differences Between Rum, Rhum Agricole, and Cachaca." VinePair, February 28, 2018. https://vinepair.com/articles/what-is-rum-rhum-agricole-cachaca/.

Offenhartz, Jake. "Literature, Murder & Prohibition: A History of Legendary West Village Speakeasy Chumley's." *Gothamist*, September 29, 2016. https://gothamist.com/food/literature-murder-prohibition-a-history-of-legendary-west-village-speakeasy-chumleys.

O'Hara, Frank. "The Day Lady Died." *Lunch Poems*. San Francisco: City Lights, 1964.

O'Hara, Frank. "Having a Coke With You." *Lunch Poems*. San Francisco: City Lights, 1964.

"Old-Fashioned." PUNCH, accessed December 16, 2019. https://punchdrink.com/recipes/old-fashioned/.

Ollman, Joe. "William Seabrook, Great Travel Writer, Terrible Human Being." *Literary Hub*, February 17, 2017. https://lithub.com/william-seabrook-great-travel-writer-terrible-human/.

Orwell, George. "A Nice Cup of Tea." *Evening Standard*, January 12, 1946.

Orwell, George. "A Nice Cup of Tea." The Orwell Foundation, accessed January 7, 2020. https://www.orwellfoundation.com/the-orwell-foundation/orwell/essays-ant-other-works/a-nice-cup-of-tea/.

"Oscar Wilde." The Absinthe Encyclopedia, accessed December 16, 2019. https://www.absinthes.com/en/absinthe-encyclopedia/the-effects-of-absinthe/oscar-wilde/.

Owen, Lauren. "Gertrude Stein, Hostess of the Parisian Literary Salon." Literary Traveler, April 4, 2007. https://www.literarytraveler.com/articles/gertrude-stein-paris/.

Pariseau, Leslie. "Why We Still Worship Hemingway at His Bars." PUNCH, July 29, 2015. https://www.punchdrink.com/articles/why-we-still-worship-hemingway-at-his-bars-paris-cuba-madrid.

Pariseau, Leslie. "Salman Rushdie Has Had Drinks With Everybody." PUNCH, September 5, 2019. https://punchdrink.com/articles/quichotte-booker-prize-salman-rushdie-drinks-with-everybody/.

"Paris-Inspired Cocktails." *Saveur*, March 18, 2015. https://www.saveur.com/gallery/Parisian-Cocktails/.

Patterson, Troy. "The Gimlet Eye: Considering the Most Unscrewupable of Cocktails." Slate, December 5, 2013. https://slate.com/human-interest/2013/12/the-gimlet-a-history-of-gin-and-roses-from-the-british-navy-to-raymond-chandler.html.

Patterson, Troy. "Martini Madness." Slate, April 8, 2013. https://slate.com/articles/life/drink/features/2013/martini _madness_tournament/sweet_16/dorothy_parker_martini_poem _why_the_attribution_is_spurious.html.

Patterson, Troy. "Three Days of Vodka with Gary Shteyngart." Slate, January 8, 2014. https://slate.com/human-interest/2014/01/gary -shteyngart-on-vodka-three-days-of-drinking-with-the-author -of-little-failure.html.

Paull, Jennifer. "Read It and Drink: A Guide to Gatsby and Alcohol." BookRiot, July 2, 2012. https://bookriot.com/2012/07/02/read-it-and -drink-a-guide-to-gatsby-and-alcohol/.

Peduzzi, Alexa. "Green Tea Arnold Palmer." Fooduzzi, accessed December 16, 2019. https://www.fooduzzi.com/2015/05/ green-tea-arnold-palmer/.

Popova, Maria. "Susan Sontag on Why Lists Appeal to Us, Plus Her Listed Likes and Dislikes." Brain Pickings, accessed December 16, 2019. https://www.brainpickings.org/2013/04/26/susan-sontag-lists -likes-dislikes/.

Porter, Katherine Anne. *Letters of Katherine Anne Porter*. New York: Atlantic Monthly, 1994.

Powell, Dannye Romine. "Eudora Welty Describes Ideal Day." *The Charlotte Observer*, August 25, 2016. https://www.charlotteobserver.com/entertainment/books/reading-matters-blog/article97231007.html.

Price, Reynolds. "A Room at Eudora's." Garden and Gun, March and April 2008. https://gardenandgun.com/feature/a-room-at-eudoras/.

"Quote Page." *Reader's Digest* 24, December 1933: 109.

"Ramos Gin Fizz - The Ultimate Guide." The Bar Cabinet, accessed November 20, 2019. https://thebarcabinet.com/features/ultimate-guides/ramos-gin-fizz/.

Rense, Sarah. "How to Make a Dark and Stormy." *Esquire*, February 22, 2019. https://www.esquire.com/food-drink/drinks/recipes/a3747/dark-and-stormy-drink-recipe/.

Reynolds, Susan Salter. "The Writing Life: Go Ask Alice." *Los Angeles Times*, November 5, 2006. https://www.latimes.com/la-bk-munro110506-story.html.

Rhind-Tutt, Louise. "Hangover Advice From Literature's Greatest Drinkers." inews, November 7, 2016. https://inews.co.uk./culture/books/hangover-advice-literatures-greatest-drinkers-532843.

"Riff Diaries: The Sherry Cobbler." PUNCH, October 25, 2013. https://punchdrink.com/articles/riff-diaries-the-sherry-cobbler/.

Robinson, Kelly. "Literature's Greatest Cocktails: 6 Inventive Libations." Book Dirt, October 2, 2011. http://bookdirtblog.blogspot.com/2011/10/literatures-greatest-cocktails-6.html.

Rodell, Besha. "Cocktail Nerdom: Happy Birthday John Steinbeck + A Recipe for the Jack Rose Cocktail." *LA Weekly*, February 27, 2013. https://www.laweekly.com/cocktail-nerdom-happy-birthday-john -steinbeck-a-recipe-for-the-jack-rose-cocktail/.

Rodgers, Lisa Townsend. "Helen Gurley Brown's Recipe to Scare Away a Man Forever." Extra Crispy, August 6, 2018. https://www.myrecipes.com/ extracrispy/helen-gurley-brown-egg-recipe-to-scare-away-a-man.

Rodwan Jr., John G. "A Drink-Man Among Drink-Men." *Open Letters Monthly*, 2008. https://www.openlettersmonthlyarchive.com/ main-articles-page/a-drink-man-among-drink-men?rq= kingsley%20amis.

Rosenberg, Emily. "A Way Out." This Recording, December 26, 2012. http://thisrecording.com/today/2012/12/26/in-which-we-embark-on -an-unsettling-endeavor.html.

Rothfuss, Patrick. "On the Making of Metheglin." Patrick Rothfuss, September 30, 2013. https://blog.patrickrothfuss.com/2013/09/on-the -making-of-metheglin/.

Rowley, Matthew. "Seamus Heaney's Sloe Gin." Rowley's Whiskey Forge, March 9, 2012. http://matthew-rowley.blogspot.com/2012/03/ seamus-heaneys-sloe-gin.html.

Russell, Iain. "Famous Whiskey Drinkers: Mark Twain." Scotchwhiskey.com, July 13, 2015. https://scotchwhisky.com/magazine/ famous-whisky-drinkers/6110/famous-whisky-drinkers-mark-twain/.

Russell, Iain. "Famous Whiskey Drinkers: Sir Kingsley Amis." Scotchwhiskey.com, June 23, 2016. https://scotchwhisky.com/magazine/famous-whisky-drinkers/9708/sir-kingsley-amis/.

Salinger, J. D., *The Catcher in the Rye.* New York: Little, Brown and Company, 1951.

Salisbury, Vanita. "Anthony Bourdain Rarely Cooks His Own Meals." *The Intelligencer, New York* magazine, December 16, 2011. http://nymag.com/intelligencer/2011/12/anthony-bourdain-rarely-cooks-his-own-meals.html.

Salisbury, Vanita. "Great Wine is Wasted on Nora Ephron." *The Intelligencer, New York* magazine, November 3, 2010. http://nymag.com/intelligencer/2010/11/21_questions_1.html.

"Salman Rushdie."*Encyclopaedia Britannica*, December 26, 2019. https://britannica.com/biography/Salman-Rushdie.

Saveur staff. "Calvados Hot Toddy." *Saveur*, November 7, 2013. https://www.saveur.com/article/recipes/calvados-hot-toddy/.

Savinon, Amanda. "Recipe: Roxane Gay's Bad Feminist Cocktail." Loyal Nana, August 10, 2018. https://www.loyalnana.com/stories-1/2018/8/10/recipe-roxane-gays-bad-feminist-cocktail.

Schaap, Rosie. "Pink Gin." *New York Times*, accessed December 11, 2019. https://cooking.nytimes.com/recipes/1016352-pink-gin.

Schaap, Rosie. "Drinking with Archibald Motley." *New York Times Magazine*, January 29, 2019. https://www.nytimes.com/2016/01/31/magazine/drinking-with-archibald-motley.html.

Schaap, Rosie. "Death in the Afternoon." Cooking, *New York Times*, accessed December 16, 2019. https://cooking.nytimes.com/recipes/1018193-death-in-the-afternoon.

Schaap, Rosie. "A San Francisco Classic: Vesuvio's Bohemian Coffee." The 6th Floor, *New York Times*, March 19, 2013. https://6thfloor.blogs.nytimes.com/2013/03/19/a-san-francisco-classic-vesuvios-bohemian-coffee/.

Schoech, Samantha, ed. *A Literary Cocktail Party: Favorite Drinks from our Favorite Writers*. San Francisco: California Bookstore Day Publishing, 2019.

Schuster, Amanda. "Mad Men and Thirsty Dames." The Alcohol Professor, April 2, 2015. https://www.alcoholprofessor.com/blog-posts/blog/2015/04/02/mad-men-and-thirsty-dames.

Scott, Sir Walter. *St. Ronan's Well*. Boston: S. H. Parker, 1824.

Sexton, Anne. "Sylvia's Death." *Poetry* magazine, 1964.

SF Insider. "What Are Some Bohemian Hangout Spots Like Vesuvio Bar in San Francisco?" *SFGate*, accessed December 16, 2019. https://sfinsider.sfgate.com/what-are-some-bohemian-hangout-spots-like-vesuvio-bar-in-san-francisco/.

Shapiro, Laura. "How Cosmopolitan's Helen Gurley Brown Taught Women to Prize Skinniness Above All Else." Quartz, September 24, 2017. https://qz.com/1085055/how-cosmopolitans-helen-gurley -brown-taught-women-to-prize-skinniness-above-all-else/.

"Sherry Cobbler." PUNCH, accessed November 20, 2019. https://punchdrink.com/recipes/sherry-cobbler/.

Simonson, Robert. *3-Ingredient Cocktails: An Opinionated Guide to the Most Enduring Drinks in the Cocktail Canon*. New York: Ten Speed Press, 2017.

Simonson, Robert. "How the Inventor of the Cosmopolitan Learned to Embrace His Most Famous Creation." *Grub Street, New York* magazine, September 19, 2016. http://www.grubstreet.com/2016/09/ meet-the-bartender-who-invented-the-cosmopolitan.html.

Simonson, Robert. "In Search of the Ultimate Hemingway Daiquiri." PUNCH, May 16, 2019. https://punchdrink.com/articles/ultimate-best -hemingway-daiquiri-cocktail-recipe/.

"Singapore Sling." PUNCH, accessed December 16, 2019. https://punchdrink.com/recipes/singapore-sling/.

"Sir Walter Scott." *Encyclopaedia Britannica*, last updated September 17, 2019. https://www.britannica.com/biography/Walter-Scott.

Small, Robin. "Philosophy & Cocktails." *Philosophy Now*, 2016, accessed December 9, 2019. https://philosophynow.org/issues/113/ Philosophy_and_Cocktails.

Spedding, Emma. "Combined Measures: Great Writers & Their Drinks." Food and Drink, *Port*, accessed December 9, 2019. https://www.port-magazine.com/food-drink/combined-measures -great-writers-their-drinks/.

Springer, Mike. "Drinking with William Faulkner: The Writer Had a Taste for The Mint Julep & Hot Toddy." Open Culture, December 29, 2011. http://www.openculture.com/2011/12/drinking_with_william _faulkner.html.

Spring, Justin. "How Alice B. Toklas Found Her Voice Through Food." Literary Hub, January 18, 2018. https://lithub.com/how-alice-b-toklas -found-her-voice-through-food/.

Steen, James. *The Kitchen Magpie*. London: Icon Books, 2014.

Stein, Gertrude. "Christian Bérard." *Portraits and Prayers*. New York: Random House, 1934.

Stein, Jordan Alexander. "How an Old Sherry Drink Defined an Era of American History." *Saveur*, December 29, 2015. https://www.saveur.com/sherry-cobbler-drink-of-an-era/.

"Stinger." PUNCH, accessed December 9, 2019. https://punchdrink.com/recipes/stinger/.

Susann, Jacqueline. *Valley of the Dolls*. New York: Grove Atlantic, 1966.

"A Taste of Tartt." *Irish Times*, November 9, 2002. https://www.irishtimes.com/news/a-taste-of-tartt-1.1125888.

Temple, Emily. "How to Make Lauren Groff and Viet Thanh Nguyen's Favorite Cocktails." Literary Hub, April 27, 2017. https://lithub.com/how-to-make-lauren-groff-and-viet-thanh-nguyens-favorite-cocktails/.

"The Ten Year Lunch: The Wit and Legend of the Algonquin Round Table: About the Algonquin." *American Masters*, PBS, November 8, 1998. http://www.pbs.org/wnet/americanmasters/the-algonquin-round-table-about-the-algonquin/527/.

Thackeray, William Makepeace. *Sketches and Travels in London*. London: Bradbury & Evans, 1856.

Thiel, Julia. "Pisco Cocktails: 1931 and Ma Serena." *Chicago Reader*, August 14, 2013. https://www.chicagoreader.com/Bleader/archives/2013/08/14/pisco-cocktails-1931-and-ma-serena.

"Think Pink Gin." Amantivino's Blog, June 1, 2011. https://amantivino.wordpress.com/2011/06/01/think-pink-gin/.

Thomson, Ian. "The Very Imperfect Ten: Tennessee Williams: Mad Pilgrimage of the Flesh." *Irish Times*, November 15, 2014. https://www.irishtimes.com/culture/books/the-very-imperfect-ten-tennessee-williams-mad-pilgrimage-of-the-flesh-1.2001154.

Thomas, Greg. "Drink of the Week: Eugene O'Neill's Gibson." Angler's Tonic, July 9, 2010. http://www.anglerstonic.com/2010/07/drink-of-the-week-eugene-oneills-gibson/.

Thomas, Greg. "Raymond Carver's Bloody Mary." Angler's Tonic, March 4, 2010. http://www.anglerstonic.com/2010/03/raymond -carvers-bloody-mary/.

Thomas, Jerry. *How to Mix Drinks: Or, The Bon-Vivant's Companion.* New York: Dick & Fitzgerald, 1862.

Thomas, Marguerite. "Random Musings on the Cocktail." Wine Review Online, December 20, 2016. http://www.winereviewonline. com/Marguerite_Thomas_on_the_Cocktail.cfm.

Thompson, Hunter S. *Fear and Loathing in Las Vegas: A Savage Journey to the Heart of the American Dream.* New York: Random House, 1972.

Tippins, Sherill. "Genius and High Jinks at 7 Middagh Street." *New York Times,* February 6, 2005. https://www.nytimes.com/2005/02/06/ nyregion/thecity/genius-and-high-jinks-at-7-middagh-street.html.

Toklas, Alice B. *The Alice B. Toklas Cook Book.* New York: Harper, 1954.

Tolentino, Jia. "The 'Sex and Rage' of Eve Babitz." *New Yorker,* July 14, 2017. https://www.newyorker.com/books/page-turner/ the-sex-and-rage-of-eve-babitz.

Tong, Alfred. *The Gentleman's Guide to Cocktails.* Australia: Hardie Grant, 2012.

Treseler, Heather. "One Long Poem." *Boston Review*, August 17, 2016. https://bostonreview.net/poetry/heather-treseler-elizabeth-bishop-foster-letters.

Updike, John. *Rabbit, Run*. New York: Alfred A. Knopf, 1960.

"Vesper." PUNCH, accessed December 9, 2019. https://punchdrink.com/recipes/vesper/.

Vinh, Tan. "A Toast to Former Seattle Times Reporter E. B. White." *Food & Wine, Seattle Times*, July 10, 2014.

"Vintage Literary—The Cocktails of Somerset Maugham." Book and Paper Arts, May 4, 2014. https://bookandpaperarts.com/the-cocktails-of-somerset-maugham/.

Vogler, Pen. "Jane Austen Recipes: White Soup." *The Telegraph*, September 26, 2013. https://www.telegraph.co.uk/foodanddrink/recipes/10323828/Jane-Austen-recipes-white-soup.html.

Wakefield, Dan. "James Baldwin Was an Honest Man and a Good Writer." Deadspin, March 30, 2017. https://thestacks.deadspin.com/james-baldwin-was-an-honest-man-and-a-good-writer-1793599858.

Walser, Lauren. "San Francisco's Vesuvio Cafe." National Trust for Historic Preservation, February 26, 2015. https://savingplaces.org/stories/historic-bars-san-franciscos-vesuvio-cafe#.XffTitVKGgR.

Warren, Richard. "A Rainy Day in Jackson for Miss Eudora Welty." Literary Traveler, July 9, 2012. https://www.literarytraveler.com/articles/edora-welty/.

"While Rome Burns Cocktail by Alexander Woollcott," *Ateriet*, Februrary 15, 2018. https://www.ateriet.com/while-rome-burns-cocktail/.

"White Fruitcake." Cookbook of the Day, December 7, 2009. https://cookbookoftheday.blogspot.com/search?q=Eudora+Welty.

"White Lady." PUNCH, accessed December 10, 2019. https://punchdrink.com/recipes/white-lady/.

Wickes, George. "A Natalie Barney Garland." *Paris Review* 61, Spring 1975. https://www.theparisreview.org/letters-essays/3870/a-natalie-barney-garland-george-wickes.

Wick, Julia. "How to Make a Gimlet Like Raymond Chandler." *LAist*, March 20, 2017. https://laist.com/2017/03/20/gimlet_like_raymond_chandler.php.

Williams, Joy. "Stranger Than Paradise." *New York Times*, February 26, 2009. https://www.nytimes.com/2009/03/01/books/review/Williams-t.html.

Wills, David S. "First Thought, Best Thought?" *Beatdom*, September 27, 2010. https://www.beatdom.com/first-thought-best-thought/.

"Wine Spodiodi." CocktailBook, accessed December 16, 2019. https://cocktailbook.com/wine-spodiodi/.

Wodehouse, P. G. "The Rummy Affair of Old Biffy." *Carry On, Jeeves*. London: Herbert Jenkins, 1925.

Wodehouse, P. G. *Uncle Fred in the Springtime*. New York: Doubleday, 1939.

Wondrich, David. "Algonquin." *Esquire*, November 5, 2007. https://www.esquire.com/food-drink/drinks/recipes/a3680/algonquin-cocktail-drink-recipe/.

Wondrich, David. "How to Make a Vodka Martini." *Esquire*, November 2, 2017. https://www.esquire.com/food-drink/drinks/recipes/a3723/vodka-martini-drink-recipe/.

Wondrich, David. "Negus." *Esquire*, November 6, 2007. https://www.esquire.com/food-drink/drinks/recipes/a3816/negus-drink-recipe/.

Woolf, Virginia. *A Room of One's Own (Annotated)*. New York: Houghton Mifflin, 2015.

Wright, John. "How to Make Metheglin." *The Guardian*, February 15, 2012. https://www.theguardian.com/lifeandstyle/wordofmouth/2012/feb/15/how-to-make-metheglin.

Yeats, William Butler. *The Collected Poems of W. B. Yeats*. New York: Scribner, 1996.

Yeomans, Rachel. "Writers and their Cocktails: Carson McCullers and Her Sonnie Boy." Lit with a Twist, accessed November 20, 2019. http://litwithatwist.com/writers-and-their-cocktails-carson -mccullers-and-her-sonnie-boy/.

Yeomans, Rachel. "Writers and their Cocktails: Tennessee Williams and the Ramos Gin Fizz." Lit with a Twist, accessed November 20, 2019. http://litwithatwist.com/writers-and-their-cocktails-tennessee -williams-and-the-ramos-fizz/.

Young, Naren. "Bison Grass Vodka Is the Stuff of Bartenders' Dreams." Eater, November 3, 2015. https://www.eater.com/drinks/2015/11/3/ 9660102/bison-grass-vodka-zubrowka.

Zavatto, Amy. "Getting Old-Fashioned with Robert Simonson and His New Cocktail Book." *Edible Manhattan*, July 23, 2014. https://www.ediblemanhattan.com/drink/getting-old-fashioned-with -robert-simonson-and-his-new-book/.

NOTES

1   Butler, "Shakespeare's Suppers."

2   Wright, "How to Make Metheglin."

3   Butler, "Shakespeare's Suppers."

4   Howe, "9 TOP Fermentation Lids for Mason Jar Fermentation."

5   "Celtic Druid's Honey Mead – Meade – Metheglin," *Food*.

6   "Negus," Jane Austen Centre.

7   Austen and Austen Lee, *A Memoir of Jane Austen*, 327.

8   Farley, London Art of Cookery, 108.

9   Martyris, "How Percy Shelley Stirred Politics into His Teacup."

10   Ibid.

11   Ibid.

12   Bieri, *Percy Bysshe Shelley: A Biography*, 357.

13   Martyris, "How Percy Shelley Stirred Politics into His Teacup."

14   Associated Press, "Poe's Death Is Rewritten as Case of Rabies."

15   Wordplay based on "The Raven," 1845.

16   Scott, *St. Ronan's Well*, 108.

17   Thackery, *Sketches and Travels in London,* 32.

18   "Sir Walter Scott," Encyclopaedia Britannica.

19   Ibid.

20   Brander, "William Makepeace Thackeray."

21   Crosariol, "A Gin Toast to Dickens, With a Twist."

22   Avey, "Eating and Drinking with Charles Dickens."

23   McAlpine, "Five Victorian Cocktails."

24   "Sherry Cobbler," PUNCH.

25   Demarest, "C'est Moi: Gustave Flaubert's 'Madame Bovary'."

26   Dyke, "Some Medical Aspects of the Life of Dante Gabriel Rossetti," 39–43.

27   Ibid.

28 "Chloral Hydrate Capsule," WebMD.

29 Dyke, 42.

30 Kubala, "7 Benefits and Uses of CBD Oil."

31 Adams, Hideous Absinthe, 150.

32 Caitlin, "Absinthe: A Conduit to Belle Epoque Paris," Behind the Bar.

33 Ibid.

34 Ibid.

35 Ibid.

36 Ibid.

37 Ciabattari, "Absinthe."

38 Ibid.

39 Adams, Hideous Absinthe, 150.

40 Russell, "Mark Twain."

41 Ibid.

42 Ibid.

43 Killius, "The Clover Club."

44 Ibid.

45 Yeats, Collected Poems of W. B. Yeats, 93.

46 Bailey, Hemingway & Bailey's Bartending Guide, 32.

47 Ibid.

48 Markel, "F. Scott Fitzgerald's Life."

49 Joyce, Dubliners, 181.

50 Toklas, Alice B. Toklas Cook Book, 261.

51 Hémard, "Milk with a Punch."

52 Woolf, A Room of One's Own, 65.

53 Hémard, "Milk with a Punch."

54 Ibid.

55 Hammonds, "Milk Punch."

56 Bicknell, ed., Selected Letters of Leslie Stephen, 26.

57 "Lifestyle and Legacy of the Bloomsbury Group," Art & Artists, Tate Museum.

58 English, "The Key to Crystal-Clear Cocktails"

59 Ibid.

60 Ibid.

61 "Quote Page," Reader's Digest, 109.

62 North and Kroch, So Red the Nose.

63 "While Rome Burns Cocktail by Alexander Woollcott," Ateriet.

64 Ollman, "William Seabrook, Great Travel Writer, Terrible Human."

65 Ibid.

66 North and Kroch, 5.

67 Ibid.

68 Lawrence, "Gourmet Highway."

69 Lanahan, "Behind the Myths of Scott and Zelda's Epic Romance."

70 Ibid.

71 Lawrence, "Gourmet Highway."

72 "George Orwell," Lovely Linda Loves Life.

73 Ibid.

74 Laing, "What Would Britain Be Without Drink?"

75 Orwell, "A Nice Cup of Tea," The Orwell Foundation.

76 Ibid.

77 Offenhartz, "Literature, Murder & Prohibition."

78 Gelb and Gelb, "Eugene O'Neill."

79 Cavanaugh, "The Truncated Drinking Career of America's Shakespeare."

80 Ibid.

81 Ibid.

82 Thomas, "Drink of the Week: Eugene O'Neill's Gibson."

83 Wick, "How to Make a Gimlet Like Raymond Chandler."

84 Chandler, *The Long Goodbye*, 19.

85 Patterson, "The Gimlet Eye."

86 Archibald, "Scotch, Martinis, and Hard-Boiled Crime."

87 "Manhattan," PUNCH,.

88 Pariseau, "Why We Still Worship Hemingway at His Bars."

89 Ibid.

90 Ibid.

91 Garret, "The Story (and Recipe) Behind the Hemingway Daiquiri."

92 Simonson, "In Search of the Ultimate Hemingway Daiquiri."

93 Greene, "The Myth Behind Hemingway's Favorite Drink."

94 Ibid.

95 Ibid.

96 North and Kroch, *So Red the Nose*, 1.

97 Moor, "Faulkner's Cocktail of Choice."

98 Springer, "Drinking with William Faulkner."

99 Williams, "Stranger Than Paradise."

100 Derk, "Flannery O'Connor's Greatest Hits."

101 Black, "Stirred Not Shaken."

102 Fleming, *Casino Royale*, 61.

103 Ibid., 60.

104 Young, "Bison Grass Vodka Is the Stuff of Bartender's Dreams."

105 "Vintage Literary," Book and Paper Arts.

106 Coetzee, "Razor's Edge."

107 "The Cocktail Hour: Evelyn Waugh," Paper and Salt.

108 Spring, "How Alice B. Toklas Found Her Voice Through Food."

109 Owen, "Gertrude Stein, Hostess of the Parisian Literary Salon."

110 Spring, "How Alice B. Toklas Found Her Voice Through Food."

111 Stein, "Christian Bérard."

112 Patterson, "Martini Madness."

113 "Algonquin Round Table," Encyclopaedia Britannica.

114 "The Ten Year Lunch," PBS.

115 Morris, "Algonquin Round Table."

116 "The Ten Year Lunch," PBS.

117 Wondrich, "Algonquin."

118 Tippins, "Genius and High Jinks at 7 Middagh Street."

119 Ibid.

120 "The Cocktail Hour: Carson McCullers," Paper and Salt.

121 Carr, *The Lonely Hunter*, 273.

122 "John Steinbeck," Encyclopaedia Britannica.

123 Rodell, "Cocktail Nerdom: Happy Birthday John Steinbeck."

124 Garret, "The Jack Rose Cocktail, a True American Classic."

125 Wills, "First Thought, Best Thought?"

126 Mazan, "Kerouac's Margarita."

127 Walser, "San Francisco's Vesuvio Cafe."

128 Celli, "Vesuvio Café."

129 Walser, "San Francisco's Vesuvio Cafe."

130 Schaap, "A San Francisco Classic."

131 "Wine Spodiodi," CocktailBook.

132 Ibid.

133 Wickes, "A Natalie Barney Garland."

134 "Natalie Barney," Sackler Center for Feminist Art.

135 Ibid.

136 Ibid.

137 Wickes, "A Natalie Barney Garland."

138 Coward, *Relative Values*, 92.

139 "El Coquetelon,"Wayfaring Seels.

140 Davis, "Chile."

141 Thiel, "Pisco Cocktails."

142 Hernandez, "Completos or Chilean Hot Dogs."

143 Collins, "Once Was Never Enough."

144 Ibid.

145 Ibid.

146 Sexton, "Sylvia's Death."

147 Rosenberg, "A Way Out."

148 Wodehouse, *Uncle Fred in Springtime,* 115.

149 "Kummel," The Whisky Exchange.

150 Wodehouse, "The Rummy Affair of Old Biffy.".

151 Curran, "She Never Went to School,"

152 Compagno, "Murder, Gin, and the Queen of Crime."

153 Schaap, "Pink Gin."

154 Bishop, "The Riverman."

155 Nurin, "The Differences Between Rum, Rhum Agricole, and Cachaça."

156 Ibid.

157 Monteiro, *Elizabeth Bishop in Brazil and After.*

158 Ibid., 55.

159 Porter, *Letters of Katherine Anne Porter*, 248.

160 Ibid., 120.

161 Fanelli, "He Too Sings America."

162 Schaap, "Drinking with Archibald Motley."

163 Maryanski, "The Aristocrat of Harlem."

164 Hughes, *The Big Sea.*

165 Bloom, *Langston Hughes*, 41.

166 "Gwendolyn Bennett," My Black History.

167 Thomson, "The Very Imperfect Ten."

168 Ibid.

169 Ibid.

170 Capote, "Truman Capote, The Art of Fiction No. 17."

171 Capote, "New Again: Truman Capote."

172 "The Cocktail Hour: E. B. White," Paper and Salt.

173 Ibid.

174 Vinh, "A Toast to Former Seattle Times Reporter E. B. White."

175 Small, "Philosophy & Cocktails."

176 Ibid.

177 Ibid.

178 Cleary, "New York Cocktail Philosophy."

179 Flynn, "New York City's White Horse Tavern."

180 Mejia, "A Brief History of the White Horse Tavern."

181 Ibid.

182 Ibid.

183 Flynn, "New York City's White Horse Tavern."

184 Higgins, "Bourbon in the P.M. with James Baldwin."

185 Ibid.

186 King, "Raymond Carver's Life and Stories."

187 "The Cocktail Hour: Raymond Carver," Paper and Salt.

188 Ibid.

189 Hughes, *A High Wind in Jamaica*, 101–2.

190 "Hangman's Blood," CocktailBook, accessed December 21, 2019, https://www.cocktailbook.com/hangmans-blood/.

191 Hughes, *A High Wind in Jamaica*.

192 Bukowski, *Factotum*.

193 Dent, "Under the Influence."

194 Ibid.

195 "Charles Bukowski," Poets' Graves.

196 Amis, *Everyday Drinking*, 83.

197 Russell, "Famous Whisky Drinkers: Sir Kingsley Amis."

198 Amis, *Everyday Drinking*.

199 Marrs, *Eudora Welty*, 348.

200 "Eudora Welty," Encyclopaedia Britannica.

201 Powell, "Eudora Welty Describes Ideal Day."

202 Warren, "A Rainy Day in Jackson for Miss Eudora Welty."

203 Ibid.

204 Halliday, "Eudora Welty's Handwritten Eggnog Recipe."

205 Ibid.

206 "Eudora Welty's White Fruit Cake," Cooking Bride.

207 "White Fruitcake," Cookbook of the Day.

208 Popova, "Susan Sontag on Why Lists Appeal to Us."

209 "Hunter S. Thompson," Encyclopaedia Britannica.

210 Carroll, *HUNTER*.

211 Thompson, *Fear and Loathing in Las Vegas*.

212 "Singapore Sling," PUNCH.

213 Thompson, *Fear and Loathing*.

214 Kress, Write Great Fiction.

215 "Norman Mailer," Encyclopaedia Britannica.

216 Mailer, *Harlot's Ghost*.

217 Gopnik, "Writers and Rum."

218 Updike, *Rabbit, Run*.

219 Zavatto, "Getting Old-Fashioned with Robert Simonson."

220 Salinger, *Catcher in the Rye*.

221 Chilton, "The Odd Life of JD Salinger."

222 Ibid.

223 Ibid.

224 Blinderman, "Christopher Hitchens."

225 Ibid.

226 Dunn, "Kir Cocktail is Cool Again."

227 Salisbury, "Great Wine is Wasted on Nora Ephron."

228 Shapiro, "How Cosmopolitan's Helen Gurley Brown Taught Women to Prize Skinniness."

229 Ibid.

230 Schuster, "Mad Men and Thirsty Dames."

231 "Making Sloe Gin Part 1," Gin Foundry.

232 Heaney, "Sloe Gin."

233 Cadogan, "Sloe Gin," BBC.

234 Angelou, "Maya Angelou, Art of Fiction No. 119."

235 Ibid.

236 "Maya Angelou," Encyclopaedia Britannica.

237 "Jackie Collins," Encyclopaedia Britannica.

238 Ibid.

239 King, "Anthony Bourdain Reveals His 'Perfect Drink.'"

240 Ibid.

241 Bourdain, "Anthony Bourdain Tells Maxim."

242 Ibid.

243 Ibid.

244 Babitz, *Sex and Rage*.

245 Jones, "To Eve Babitz."

246 Ibid.

247 Ibid.

248 Cheh, "Looking at Los Angeles."

249 Laing, "'Every Hour a Glass of Wine.'"

250 Reynolds, "The Writing Life."

251 Mickelbart, "Joan Didion On Stage."

252 Greg, "19th Century Poet Lord Byron," Daily Grail.

253 Ibid.

254 Ibid.

255 McInerney, "Good Wine and Fax Machines."

256 McInerney, "How Jay McInerney Combined His Love of Writing and Wine."

257 Ibid.

258 Ibid.

259 Ibid.

260 Pariseau, "Salman Rushdie Has Had Drinks with Everybody."

261 "Salman Rushdie," Encyclopaedia Britannica.

262 Murakami, *Hard-Boiled Wonderland*, 240.

263 Maynard, "Straight Up."

264 Hiatt, "Haruki Murakami's Homecoming."

265 Erlich, "How I Get It Done."

266 Simonson, "How the Inventor of the Cosmopolitan Learned to Embrace His Most Famous Creation."

267 Bushnell, "Swingin' Sex? I Don't Think So."

268 Simonson, "How the Inventor of the Cosmopolitan Learned to Embrace His Most Famous Creation."

269 Bushnell, *Sex and the City*.

270 Aran, "Making History."

271 Benfer, "Gertrude and Alice."

272 Ibid.

273 Greenberg, "Natalie Clifford Barney."

274 Ibid.

275 Ibid.

276 Fitch, *Sylvia Beach and the Lost Generation*, 72.

277 "A Taste of Tratt," Irish Times.

278 Coffey, "Interview: The Very, Very Private Life of Ms. Donna Tartt."

279 Graham, "Black Velvet Cocktail."

280 Coffey, "Interview."

281 Anolik, "The Secret Oral History of Bennington."

282 Ellis, *The Rules of Attraction*.

283 Ellis, *Less Than Zero*.

284 Anolik, "The Secret Oral History of Bennington."

285 Ellis, *White*.

286 "10 Things Every J.K. Rowling Fan Should Know," Cosmopolitan.

287 Lee, "JK Rowling Unveils New Website."

288 Chee and Crowley, ed., "Author Alexander Chee."

289 Ibid.

290 Bainbridge, "Writer Alexander Chee on Classic Cocktails."

291 Lee, "Interview with Min Jin Lee."

292 Ibid.

293 James and Crowley, ed., "Marlon James Has No Times for Fussy Cocktails."

294 Temple, "How to Make Lauren Groff and Viet Thanh Nguyen's Favorite Cocktails."

295 Ibid.

296 Patterson, "Three Days of Vodka with Gary Shteyngart."

297 Fitzgerald, "Drinking with Novelist Gary Shteyngart."

298 Ibid.

299 Ibid.

300 Gay, *An Untamed State*.

301 Savinon, "Roxane Gay's Bad Feminist Cocktail."

302 Ibid.

303 Brodesser-Akner and Crowley, ed., "Taffy Brodesser-Akner Loves a Good Breakfast Salad."

304 Ibid.

305 Temple, "How to Make Lauren Groff and Viet Thanh Nguyen's Favorite Cocktails."

306 Kwon and Crowley, ed., "Author R. O. Kwon Spends Her Days Off with Tacos."

307 Ibid.

308 Kendrick, "I'm Never Drinking Again."

309 Nastasi, "12 Hangover Cures."

310 Ibid.

311 Dubow, "Hangover Cures."

312 Rhind-Tutt, "Hangover Advice."

313 Ibid.

314 Nastasi, "12 Hangover Cures."